Behind with the Laundry and Living off Chocolate

Life changing strategies for busy women

Lynette Allen

First published by

Crown House Publishing Ltd
Crown Buildings, Bancyfelin, Carmarthen, Wales, SA33 5ND, UK
www.crownhouse.co.uk

and

Crown House Publishing LLC
4 Berkeley Street, 1st Floor, Norwalk, CT 06850, USA
www.CHPUS.com

First published 2004: reprinted 2004

British Library Cataloguing-in-Publication Data
A catalogue entry for this book is available from the British Library.

ISBN 1904424392

LCCN 2004106209

Printed and bound in the UK by
The Cromwell Press
Trowbridge
Wiltshire

Behind with the Laundry and Living off Chocolate

For

Nick, Georgie and Barney

Acknowledgements

Where to start? If I start at the beginning of the story, I would like to thank Steve Wright and Janey Lee Grace for inviting me on to the *Steve Wright in the Afternoon Show* on BBC Radio 2 one very sunny July day in 2003. Caroline Lenton heard the show and e-mailed me to ask if I would write a book for Crown House Publishing. So, a huge thanks, Steve and the crew and a massive thank you to Caroline and everyone at Crown House Publishing for giving me the chance to fulfil a dream. Many thanks to Fiona Spencer Thomas for all your late nights spent editing this book with me; your guiding hand has been much appreciated and I've enjoyed every step. Apologies and thanks are owed to Tom Fitton who designed the cover; I know I got your brain wracked on this one! Thank you as well to photographer Paul Keevil; what a pleasure it is to work with you.

As for my coaching journey, there are two people who are responsible for helping me to become the coach I am today—Jonathan Jay and Gabrielle Blackman-Shepphard. Their vision, trust and massive support during my learning curve gave me not only a whole host of new opportunities to shine but also the ability to help others shine too. Thanks too to Nic Rixon for building my courage and confidence when I needed it along the way, and big thank you's to all my clients who have given me such inspirational stories to tell.

A million thanks to Mum, Dad, Craig and Tracey for all their patience and encouragement as I babbled on, and great thanks to every single one of my friends who all give me so much support and love enabling me to be the very best I can. Lastly, all my deepest love goes to my husband, the gorgeous Nick, whose love, trust, patience and adoration gives me wings to fly—thank you.

How to use this book

Hands up if you've ever shouted "STOP THE WORLD, I WANT TO GET OFF!"—well this is your chance to make that saying a reality. This book is now your very own sanctuary, a place where you can go when life seems just a bit too tough, a place where you can find the answers to life's problems. Inside is a host of tips that you can make your very own. By reading and absorbing them, you'll be giving yourself the unadulterated luxury of thinking about you!

With these realistic, workable, tried and tested methods, your friends will want to know how you can laugh when your life is in chaos, make effective choices in the face of adversity and trust yourself that, whatever happens, you'll be OK! Understand the real power of being a woman and having it all. If you're behind with the laundry, lacking inspiration, desperate to get some kind of control over your life and living off coffee and chocolate, this book is especially for you!

You can dip in when you most need support and you don't have to plough your way through it to find the part that applies to you. Simply look up the tip that is closest to your situation or issue of the day and you'll immediately have a strategy that you may not have considered before. Adapt each suggestion to suit you and, at last, you'll have solutions that really complement both your individuality and your hectic lifestyle! You'll find a whole series of complex and serious subjects discussed in a light-hearted and humorous way, using down-to-earth examples of real women who have overcome all sorts of fears and issues. The stories you will read are real and the tips I have illustrated can bring about huge changes in people's lives, proving that change really doesn't need to be scary.

Use this book to consider how you run your life, the habits you have developed and your patterns of behaviour, both consciously and subconsciously. When I see clients for the first time, I talk to them about three things: the role of the subconscious mind, female intuition and dehydration. The subconscious has a bigger impact on your behaviour patterns and actions than you might think and the power of a woman's intuition is largely underrated as a guide, both in business and personally. Finally, it may seem odd that dehydration is on the list but its effect can be very debilitating and I will explain why. These three issues are all covered, giving you the opportunity to take control of your body and your life in a positive and healthy way.

Written especially for women, *Behind with the Laundry and Living off Chocolate* recognises that we girls have it tough! Yep, we wanted equality and we got it, we wanted careers and we got them—all great stuff—but no one realised that we would still have to fulfil our traditional womanly roles on top of these new challenges. No one can take away the pressure we put on ourselves to hoist all this on board and pull it off perfectly! We've got career paths to follow, targets to beat plus the gym to get to. We're the ones that worry about eating healthily, being a sexy wife, multitalented mother, adventurous girlfriend, great best friend and a thoughtful daughter. We remember the birthdays, do the shopping, dress to impress and run the kids to school! What's more, we're meant to do all this and more without getting emotional, stressed, worn out, tearful or downright hysterical!

Well, it's time to get smart and take a breather. If, secretly, you know you could be making much more of yourself and your existence on this planet, or if you just want a few tips to deal with the day-to-day trials of living, you've picked up the right book. From lifting those heavy guilt pangs to setting personal boundaries, from altering your body language so you can get what you want and learning how and why it is so important to think positively, this book contains inspirational and creative tips to help make your day, week, month and year run just that little bit smoother!

Use them as you please: either read right through the book, one by one, or use your intuition a little. Do this by holding the book in both hands and concentrating on a specific problem. Once you've done that, simply open up the book at any page and start reading. The chances are that you opened a page containing a strategy that may well help you. Remember that when using your intuition, the subconscious mind works in illogical ways, so think about how that strategy could help your particular problem. It might even be glaringly obvious. Alter each tip to suit your personal situation but take the inspiration and use the ideas as your secret weapon for success.

Contents

What, this old thing?

Learn how to take compliments with pride

Do you blush every time someone pays you a compliment? Do you put yourself down before your friend even finishes her sentence? You're not alone ... but this will give you something to think about.

Oh go on ... just take it! You wouldn't think it would be so difficult would you? Nearly every woman I have ever coached though has, at some point, brought up the fact that she finds it hard to accept a compliment. Why is it that whenever someone of whatever sex says, "You look nice today!" we feel we have to throw it back at them with a self-deprecating answer like, "What, this old thing?" or "God no, I look awful!" What is it that physically stops us from just smiling graciously and proudly saying "thank you!"?

From chief executives to mothers bringing up small children, the story is just the same. When I've asked my clients what stops them taking a compliment, the answers range from feeling guilty and embarrassed about looking good, to simply not believing the compliment was really meant in the first place.

Accepting a compliment is not about being vain or showing off, it's about feeling good about yourself, and everyone is allowed to do that. People who show off often do so at the expense of others. They outshine those less confident on purpose, knowing they will steal the limelight. People who are vain do the same. So preoccupied are they about how they look, they forget that other people have feelings and often fail to notice when anyone else looks good. On the other hand, people who accept compliments come across as self-confident in a way that makes other people feel good too. They don't aim to steal the show but want you to share the limelight with them.

Sometimes my clients say that even when their hair, make-up and stomachs seem to be behaving themselves, they would never admit to anyone that they know they're looking gorgeous. The reason why some women find it hard to take compliments varies. Sometimes it's due to the way they were brought up and sometimes it's that nagging feeling that they're not quite good enough. Others think that, by putting themselves down, they'll make others feel better in the process! Whatever the reason, though, if you've got self-deprecation off to a fine art, I'm here to remind you just how fabulous you really are. It's definitely time for us girls to stick together and start taking those compliments with our heads held high.

One of my clients, Amy, was surprised at how just one word altered her view of herself. Amy is fantastic at praising her friends and family. She always makes sure people around her feel special and loved. Giving compliments is one way she does this, but accepting them is another matter completely. As we spoke about this issue, Amy realised it was her need for perfection in her life that stopped her accepting compliments. No matter how good she felt or how great she looked, she was always convinced that she could do better, be better, look better. In her eyes, she just was never good enough and, when people complimented her, it just seemed to make her feel worse about herself.

During one of our sessions, I asked that the next time Amy received a compliment, she react to it differently. I asked her to do two things, smile and then say "thank you". I asked her to do whatever it took to keep her mouth firmly closed to stop the familiar barrage of self-deprecating nonsense that usually followed. Amy reluctantly agreed. It wasn't easy. In fact, it was so hard that she literally bit her lip after the word "thank you" came out in a bid to stop herself saying something like, "Oh, it was only five pounds in the sale!" She did do it though, and after every single compliment, she just smiled and said, "Thank you."

Throughout the week, her friends started to comment on how relaxed and happy she looked. Without even realising it, by accepting compliments, Amy was already reconditioning her mind to accept that she was good enough. She suddenly found that she didn't have to work so hard at being perfect and slowly began to acknowledge that she was doing absolutely fine just as she was. This is powerful stuff and it changed Amy's concept of herself. It also changed how others saw her and, ultimately, brought her a new-found friend in herself. Finally, she relaxed and started to really appreciate who she was and what she had achieved, just by being herself.

If you see a bit of yourself in Amy, whatever your reason for deflecting compliments, the next time someone says something flattering, think for just a millisecond before you open your mouth to put yourself down. There's no harm in someone telling you that you look great! People only really ever give compliments with sincerity, so don't throw them back in their face—enjoy the fact that someone admires you and thinks you have great taste or look wonderful. The rich and famous love to be adored and complimented—it's not a bad thing—so follow their example, let compliments make your day and let them lift your spirits. Just say "thank you".

How well do you take care of yourself?

Time to put yourself first and look after number one

Do you seem to come at the bottom of a very long list of priorities? Do you compromise your dreams, so someone else can live theirs? Well, maybe it's time to look after you for a change ...

I have clients that say, "I never thought this would happen to me." Throughout their twenties, when they only had themselves to look after, they did just that, thought about themselves. They made time for their friends, had nights out with the girls, painted their toenails and spent hours in the bath with their faces covered in some gooey, smelly substance that promised eternal youth. But as they got older and took on more responsibilities, life changed, priorities changed and other people seemed more important. Somehow they found themselves at the very bottom of the list. Suddenly, those relaxing long baths and hilarious nights out seemed a vague and distant memory.

This tip is for women all over the world. Whatever you do, whether you go out to work, bring up children (or both!) think about how you take care of yourself and how you should put yourself first. I firmly believe that you have to take care of you first because, when you do, you have the energy and vitality to take care of everyone else and you're much nicer to be around.

Think about the structure of the word "yourself". When you look at it, it's really two words—"your" and "self" put together. If someone said to you, take care of your dog, you presumably would be the owner of the dog. As a responsible owner, one would hope that you'd feed it well, walk it every day, give it lots of attention and make sure it stayed happy and healthy. What you wouldn't do is forget to feed it, never take it out to play and feed it chocolates and coffee if it whined. Thinking differently yet? You own your "self"! It's yours! You can do with it whatever you wish. Make sure you realise this though—it's the only one you have. You just can't do the wrong thing all the time and order a new one when the old one breaks down—

wouldn't that be nice! No, this one—this body, this mind, this "self"—is yours to keep and you probably want it to last a long time.

So be honest here and think, how well do you look after your "self"? Do you give yourself plenty of exercise, feed yourself only the freshest food? Do you pay yourself attention when you need it, praise yourself when you've done something brilliantly, all to make sure you stay healthy and happy, physically, emotionally and spiritually?

I've coached many women who cope by putting other people first. When I put it to them that "they" are more important than everyone else, I'm not always popular. Children come first they say, my colleagues rely on me, my parents always looked after me, now it's my turn to look after them—all of which is true—but before any of those people comes you. If you are not OK in the first place, if you are not healthy and happy, how can you possibly give someone else your time, attention and strength?

If those around you rely on you, then give them a strong, happy and healthy person to rely on. Give your children a role model to follow, not a mother who has worn herself into the ground and looks awful, just to give them designer clothes and the latest toys. Teach them how to look after themselves by your example.

If you're not putting yourself first, what are you teaching your daughter? Are you teaching her that she will have to come last when she's a grown-up? What about your son? Are you teaching him that any woman he meets in the future is going to treat him like a king at the expense of her own health and happiness? Future daughter-in-laws will thank you and your daughters will grow up knowing their worth and valuing themselves.

They deserve to understand how to put themselves first as adults too—so this week, how could you look after yourself better? What example do you need to set? Make a list of five things that you could do this week that mean you go straight to the top of that list? Put yourself first and take care of yourself.

Set boundaries and find your parallel universe!

Read how to stop people taking advantage of your good nature

Are you feeling the strain in a relationship because you feel your so-called "friend" is over-stepping the mark? Maybe someone at work is taking advantage of your good nature? Perhaps you've been carrying a colleague long enough and your frustration is reaching breaking point? Then you probably need to set a few bound-aries, which needn't be as alarming as it sounds!

We all have boundaries, don't we? Those invisible lines that sting us like little electric shocks when people cross them! They don't sting the "crossee" of course. In fact, half the time, the lines are so invisible that the person isn't even aware of their existence. If they keep overstep-ping the mark, though, they leave us silently smouldering until, one day, we decide that enough is enough and end up exploding at said "crossee" as they look on in amazement because we're acting so weird and out of character!

Your patience can only be expected to stretch so far. Surely, they must have seen it coming? They must have noticed. They must have realised they were impinging on your space and taking very risky chances in the process … mustn't they?

Well, not really! Chances are, they had no idea there was even a boundary there … not if you didn't tell them. By the way, we're not just talking emotional boundaries; physical boundaries are just as important. Emotionally, people know they can take advantage of your good nature, sometimes truly believing that you don't mind being their "personal aide" in life. Physically, people who intrude on your personal space are encroaching on your emotions too. As a general rule, your personal space is about an arm's length away from your body and that boundary should be crossed by invitation only. People who cross it without being invited are likely to make us feel invaded and threatened.

So where exactly are your boundaries? Do *you* even know? A farmer clearly marks out his land. I bet you know where your property finishes and your neighbour's starts. So why don't you know where your personal boundaries are?

One of my clients, Laura, had a colleague, Sarah, who was unlucky in love to say the least. She was completely besotted with the gorgeous Mark but hadn't the courage to do anything about it. Every day, Laura was faced with a barrage of what Mark said or didn't say, what he really meant and what he might have meant. Laura wanted to help. She wanted to be sympathetic and she certainly didn't want to upset her already fragile friend, but she was running out of patience fast. Laura sometimes felt like Mark was their only topic of conversation and any-thing she had to say to Sarah was generally dismissed as unimportant and irrelevant by comparison. Laura was starting to feel like her only role in their friendship was to psychoanalyse the gorgeous Mark and, quite frankly, Laura wished that the gorgeous Mark would psychodisappear into a parallel universe somewhere! With Laura's patience wearing thin, at my suggestion, she agreed to put a boundary in place—the fifteen-minute rule.

I asked her to sit down with Sarah, be totally honest with her and make a deal. The deal was this: Laura's love-sick friend had just fifteen minutes to coo over the gorgeous Mark and then they had to change the subject completely. It didn't matter what they spoke about but it had to be totally different.

One week later and a very different situation had evolved. Laura's friend had agreed to stick to the fifteen-minute rule. After which, Sarah asked about Laura's weekend, what she'd been up to and how she was feeling. They realised that they had much more interesting things to talk about than the gorgeous Mark. In fact, it seems that the gorgeous Mark faded into that parallel universe that Laura had previously wished for!

So, who's treading all over your boundaries? Do they even know they're doing it? Think about your boundaries and be really specific. Where exactly is your line and who consistently crosses it? If you were the type of person that had clear and visible boundaries, what would you be doing differently?

Learn where your invisible boundaries are and consider how you can make them more visible. Think about when you are being taken advantage of and think about how you can tell friends and family that you now have boundaries and you don't expect them to be crossed. You can even use your intuition here. What do you feel, instinctively, is the right thing to do? Do you need to confront the person overstepping the mark and make it clear that you've had enough? Maybe you need to be more subtle in your approach and be ready with a different answer next time your friend calls and that familiar "Would you just …?" question pops up. Stop for a minute and take yourself off somewhere quiet. Go for a walk round the block to clear your head and use your intuition. Ask yourself, "What is the most effective way for me to deal with this?" and whatever comes into your head, think about how you can use it as a solution.

Putting boundaries in place really doesn't have to be confrontational. In fact, when you start to draw clearer lines, your friends are very likely to follow your example and do the same. People generally respect boundaries, so don't be afraid to stand up for yours!

Let's get passionate!

Life feeling a bit dreary? This will get you thinking

*What turns you on? Where does your passion lie? Does the washing, ironing, cooking and cleaning always come before the stuff you'd love to be doing? What is it that you **absolutely** must do before leaving this planet? If your passions are at the bottom of a very long list, stop the excuses and do something about it.*

It seems to me that, in this life, there are things that we'd all *like* to do, things that we all *should* be doing and things that other people tell us we really *need* to do. So many of my clients forget about the things that they absolutely *have* to do before their final "checkout".

Have you ever thought about what it is that you absolutely *have* to do? If you thought about it for a moment, if you were to make up an "absolutely have to" list, what would you write down? Swimming with dolphins? Trekking in Outer Mongolia? Singing? Painting? Dancing? Put pen to paper now … Go on, get a pen and blank sheet of paper and spend five minutes just scribbling away. You needn't show anyone, you needn't tell anyone; this is your own private and personal wish list. Write everything down that you absolutely must do in this life. Why? Because these are the things that fuel us. Your passions give you the energy to continue when life gets tough. When you do things you're passionate about, you end up with amazing stories to tell your grandchildren, and other people just can't help but stand back in amazement at your courage and energy for life!

You'll be immensely proud of yourself for doing, accomplishing and achieving whatever it is you set your mind to, and in the process you'll inspire your friends and family to do the same. Everything on this list will boost your self-confidence and strengthen your self-esteem.

I wrote an "absolutely have to" list when I took control of my own life. I wrote down everything that I'd love to be able to say I had achieved, and at the very top of the list was my wish to become a professional dancer. It was a long time ago now but dancing was in my blood. I was passionate about it and I took the decision to do everything in my power to make sure it happened. I had to get it out of my system. Dancing had been my love since I was little but a car crash and a lot of back pain seemed to mark the end of my dream before it had even got off the ground. After finding an amazingly talented and dedicated teacher, and pairing up with my dance partner and now very dear friend Chris, both I and they worked very hard and patiently to help me develop the strength and technique I needed.

I gave up my job to make time for even more dance classes. I would start at 9am and finally finish at the gym with Chris at 9pm. Most mornings I would swim a mile or so. I was a girl with a mission and my determination paid off. I ended up dancing all over Greece and performing to audiences of sometimes thousands. I didn't do it for the money, I barely made enough to live on, I did it because I was passionate! I gave up the excuses and did what it took to bring my dreams to life.

This was a life-changing event for me but being passionate doesn't have to be extreme. It could be that you have a burning passion to be a great gardener, to watch seeds grow and enter your prize vegetables in competitions. It could be taking up riding or skiing. What it is doesn't actually matter. What matters is the passion.

Once my clients write their "absolutely have to" lists, what happens afterwards is quite amazing … They grow! They grow in stature, they grow in spirit, they get excited and they even start to look different. When people have a passion, they start planning. They make phone calls, they gather information, they leave the excuses behind and they look forward. When people decide to learn something new, the value is not only in acquiring a new skill but in learning new things about themselves. Sometimes they have far more emotional strength and determination than they ever realised, deepening their whole personal journey in life.

Whatever's on your "absolutely have to" list, pick one thing to concentrate on, put a plan into practice, save up the money, make new contacts, ask around and just do it. Get passionate, drop the excuses and don't give up!

Watch out—subconscious at work

Could you be sabotaging your own success?

Do you know how your subconscious mind works? Are you aware of the huge part it plays in your life? With this information, you really can do anything you put your mind to.

I have come to realise that the subconscious mind is not only responsible for the mechanical workings of our bodies and our state of health but also for our way of thinking, the habits we form and our actions.

This was an important lesson for me and it is one of the very first things I teach people. I believe my clients need this basic understanding if they are to direct their lives properly.

In simplistic terms, your conscious mind is the part of your brain that gets you to work on time (with any luck) and makes day-to-day decisions. It's the part of your brain that does all the thinking (and worrying).

Your subconscious mind behaves in a very different way, and once you understand how it works, you are then ready to make sure you get it working for you instead of against you.

The subconscious is a powerful entity and we still have much to learn about it but we do know this—it listens. It sits quietly and takes in every single word you say in its literal sense. It absorbs every word you hear and every single image you see. It stores all this information for use at a later date.

Your subconscious mind is completely nonjudgemental: it doesn't understand the right information from wrong and it can't tell the difference between good material and bad. When it receives messages, it searches way, way back into its deepest memory for proof that what it's just heard is correct.

If, for instance, as a child, you were told by your teacher that you were not very good at Maths, of course you were disappointed, but you got over it, right? Wrong! Your subconscious has now accepted, without question, a very simple fact—you can't do Maths. From now on, every time you try to work out a mathematical problem and get it wrong, your subconscious sends a message to your conscious mind that you got it wrong because you're useless at Maths! If and when you get a mathematical problem right, you are so convinced of your shortcoming, that your brain dismisses your achievement and tells you it was too easy or just a fluke. We've all done this: even when we do things correctly, we automatically tend to dismiss our achievements. How mad is that?

From birth, whether you realise it or not, your subconscious has been programmed to think in a certain way. In this case and, unfortunately, in a lot of others, the programming is negative. The good news, though, is that because you can programme your subconscious negatively, you can also programme it positively. Don't sabotage your success in life by choosing to programme your subconscious in a negative way; instead, make your subconscious your friend and feed it with quality thoughts —all the time. As its payback, your subconscious will reward you with a quality life, one that you love, and you'll learn to be proud of yourself and your achievements, however great or small.

Learn to take notice of the negative thoughts you have and the words you use to describe yourself. When you're wandering around muttering to yourself, catching your image in the mirror, for instance, make sure you're thinking nice things about yourself. There's a motto I use—"Treat yourself like your best friend". If you wouldn't say it to your best friend, don't say it to yourself! Once you make a decision to recognise your own negative language, you'll start to notice other people's negative vocabulary. Instinctively, you'll start to see just how much damage people can do to themselves just by thinking negatively. From now on, make a pact with yourself never to finish a negative sentence again. This is powerful stuff and you deserve only the very best.

Make a concerted effort to replace negative thoughts with positive alternatives. This isn't just happy clap-trap, this really matters and it's something that every woman should know and do. When I ask my clients to start repeating positive statements, they tell me they don't believe them. This is because they may have spent twenty or thirty years training their minds to believe something negative and, at this stage, this exercise is literally about re-writing the script in their subconscious. It truly doesn't matter whether you believe it or not initially, but you will with practice. Some of my clients feel totally different about themselves after only one or two weeks of banishing negative language. If you repeat your positive alternative over and over again, your subconscious mind will eventually learn that the affirmations it is now hearing are the truth.

Work out exactly what you say to yourself that's negative and then write down the exact opposite. Make sure that your subconscious really gets the message. Your subconscious sees things out of the corner of your eye and notices what your conscious mind doesn't necessarily pick up. Your subconscious takes in information in all kinds of ways, so have fun with your new-found confidence. Write messages to yourself in as many places as you will see them: on the dashboard in your car; leave a note inside your diary or in the corner of the bathroom mirror. Give yourself the very best of opportunities. The more times you see it, think it and say it, the more likely your subconscious is to take notice of it. In no time at all, your positive alternative will be the truth.

Using your subconscious mind is more than just wishing for a situation. It is about really seeing a situation in your mind, time and time again, until the vision is ingrained there, until your mind and emotions are perfectly in tune with how it would actually feel to be in that situation.

When I started coaching, I had a fantastic mentor coach who fuelled me with encouragement and positive thinking. When we first met, Gabrielle immediately asked me why I wanted to be a coach. I told her that I wanted to be an inspiration to others. I felt that I had achieved so much in my life so far, and my aim in coaching was to show other people that they can achieve exactly what they want too. From that moment on, she called me her "little inspirational coach"! She explained that, in order to become an inspirational coach, I had to believe that I was one. Of course, my first question was, "How on earth do I do that when I've only just started learning?" She explained how the subconscious mind worked and asked me to use my subconscious mind in the way that I have just described to you. Doing exactly as I was told, I repeated, "I am an inspirational coach" hundreds of times each day, while I was waiting for the kettle to boil or listening to jangling "hold" music on the phone or when I was in a traffic jam. Time doing nothing soon turned into time training my mind. That, she said, coupled with my determination and passion to become skilled at my craft, was sure to get me there. She told me that what I put out into the world would come back, and I am fortunate to say that it has done, many times over.

If you were your best friend, what would you want for yourself? What would you want your best friend to believe about herself? Start treating yourself like your best friend and get thinking … positively!

Green Cross Code for women—stop, listen and act!

A great decision-making tool — your intuition

Do you ever get a nagging feeling about someone or something? A feeling that you know something just isn't right but you have no reasonable explanation for it? That tiny feeling could well be your intuition ... Read this tip to learn how to use it and rely on it properly.

We girls are meant to be really good at this—listening to our intuition. I was lucky enough to be brought up by a mother who had a strong sense of intuition. She thought it was important to make both my brother and I aware of it. From a very young age, we were encouraged to listen to our intuition and act on our instincts. This is exactly what I now encourage my clients to do. Intuition is a kind of in-built radar system we all have. It is there to be listened to. It's there to help steer us in the right direction but, do you use yours? Maybe you don't believe there is such a thing? Well, I have news for you: every one of us has the gift of intuition and, when used properly, it is a highly effective decision-making tool.

Intuition is such a tiny, quiet whisper that it often goes unheard. It's that fleeting thought that flew through your head at a hundred miles an hour and you forgot to catch. Before you blinked it was gone but, can you remember what it was trying to tell you? No! In an age where we are bombarded with so much information—junk mail, phone calls, text messages, e-mails, television, newspapers, advertising—we seem to have so much information to process that it's really amazing we don't forget more. Among all this chaos, how on earth are you meant to hear your intuition as well? Simple really: the trick is to quieten the chaos. I call it the "Green Cross Code for women".

Imagine you're at a party. There are hundreds of people there, all laughing, chatting and trying to talk to each other above the music blaring out. You can just about see someone at the other end of the room between the heads of people jostling in front of you. Now imagine that person is trying to get a message to you, by whispering … Starting to get the picture? You have more chance of being picked as the next astronaut to be launched into outer space as you have of really hearing that message. Now, imagine this scenario. You're standing on a chair, the music's been turned off and everyone is quiet ... It might still be tricky but you'd stand much more chance of actually getting the whispered message from your friend at the other end of the room. Well, your friend at the back of the room is your intuition. In order to hear what your intuition is trying to tell you, you need to clear your mind of all its noise.

There are likely to be plenty of things clogging up that space between your ears—an argument you had with someone earlier maybe; the worry about a speech you have to give later in the week; wondering where on earth you're going to find the time to buy your best friend's birthday present. Here's what to do. Take a pen and paper and write down the contents of your mind. Literally, spill out everything, absolutely everything that you're worried about or that you mustn't forget to do. Empty your mental "to do" list and take those thoughts out of your conscious mind. It will help you to stop and be still. Feeling calmer already? Now, close your eyes for five minutes. Set your alarm if you're scared you'll fall asleep but, if you do nothing else today, take the time to empty your mind, stop and breathe.

I'm not saying that this is easy but this is a vital exercise for anyone hoping to hear their intuition. While you're day-dreaming, be aware of the ideas that come into your mind and acknowledge them.

When you open your eyes and come back to the land of the living, remember your thoughts. It could well be that you've thought of a different way of solving a problem, an alternative way to deal with a difficult person, or you might even have thought of someone you haven't spoken to for ages. Acting on your intuition means making decisions when there are no real facts on which to base those decisions. It is literally just a hunch. You know when you've done something that turned out wrong and you'd always had a bad feeling about it? That's when you kick yourself for not having listened to your instinct. The thing about intuition is that, if you're not in tune with it, you only realise that it was tapping you on the shoulder and trying to tell you something *after* the event. What I am trying to say, is that it is possible to capture those hunches in time for you to use them. It just takes a little practice.

Intuition is a kind of clarity you have about what decision to make that usually makes no more sense to you than it does to anyone else. It is well known in our house, for instance, that if my mum has a "feeling", you trust her. Intuition is not always easy to follow. For example, she once had a very strong feeling about a car that my granddad gave to my father to use for a long journey. He proudly pulled up in it outside our house and it started a huge family argument when my mother said she didn't like it. She couldn't explain what it was about the car that she didn't like but she was definitely not happy about my dad taking it on a long trip. As it happened, on this occasion my mum's hunch was ignored and he set off on his journey. He had a bad accident on that trip and was very lucky not to have been injured more seriously.

Trust your intuition and try to tune into your radar system. It will *lead* you in the right direction. When you get a hunch about something, don't dismiss it, follow it up and trust your instinct or you might regret it.

Eliminate problems!

A different approach to finding solutions

Do you see problems as negative situations? Do you find it hard to see through the panic when something major has gone wrong? Well, you're certainly not the only one. This tip could very well be your answer to a panic-free zone.

Several years ago, a dear friend of mine, Tim, called me. "I have a situation that I'd like to talk through with you," he said.

"A situation?" I replied. "What do you mean?"

"Well, I have a problem, but I've eliminated the word 'problem' from my vocabulary. I now choose to call problems 'situations'. It takes the panic away!"

Tim isn't a life coach, but he might do well to consider becoming one. I'd never come across someone before who had chosen to eliminate the word "problem" from their vocabulary. Ever since then, I've used this exercise myself and with my clients to great effect.

When a situation occurs, we immediately view that situation in either a negative or positive way. We also condition our subconscious into thinking that certain situations will produce certain outcomes, be they negative or positive. We do this, based on our past experiences and fears. When we call something a "problem", we cease to be able to find solutions easily. We paint the situation in a negative light and it takes a lot more effort for us to see the good in it. Obviously, some situations are much more serious than others but, generally speaking, we all encounter some kind of situation during the course of the day, from which something good can come.

A few years ago, a client of mine, Amanda, went into work as usual. Within the hour, she was being escorted off the premises—she had been made redundant. She was upset, in shock and hadn't the first clue what she was going to do. She called me in a terrible state. During the conversation, I encouraged her to avoid using the word "problem" and any other negative language for that matter. I asked her to explain the situation exactly as it was, at that moment. I then asked her to imagine that this was the best news she had had all week. I asked her what her reaction to this situation would be if that were the case. Amanda found this very difficult. How could this be the best news ever, after she had been treated so badly? I urged her to humour me and answer my question. She went silent for a while. Then came her answer. If this was the best news she had heard all week, she would be feeling a certain amount of relief. She had worked very hard and was very loyal to her company but felt that, despite her efforts, she was being treated differently to her male colleagues. If the truth be told, she had been getting more and more unhappy and anxious about going into work. She admitted that she would have found it very hard to pluck up the courage to leave and make a career change. If anything positive had come out of this situation, it would be the fact that she could now take the time to consider a new direction. It could be her chance to do something totally different with her life.

This is when Amanda started to move emotionally. A breakthrough at last. The tone of her voice changed, her speech became more animated and the panic disappeared. Amanda now saw this situation as an opportunity to alter the way she lived her life. Her intuition, she told me, had been screaming at her that she needed to leave but fear of not finding another job had stopped her conscious mind from taking any notice of her intuition. She had buried it for a long time and now her redundancy had finally given her freedom.

Consequently, what had seemed like devastating news at first, became a new and positive challenge. Amanda is now a qualified nurse, loving her job and getting more satisfaction out of one afternoon than she ever did in one month at her previous job.

Be inspired and take the panic away, eliminate the word "problem" from your vocabulary and give yourself the opportunity to see a whole new set of options. Don't take my word for it—try it and see.

Getting personal with your values

A strategy to help you make difficult decisions with ease

Do you find it difficult to make decisions? Do you end up asking everyone else's opinion and wind up even more confused? Well, if you knew what values mattered to you most, that could all be a thing of the past.

Honesty, trust, freedom, happiness, fairness, passion ... deep and meaningful, don't you think? Knowing and understanding your personal values is powerful knowledge.

Our personal values govern how we live our lives. Most of us try to act with integrity, for instance, and most people try to be fair when dealing with others. But have you ever thought which values mean the most to you? "How," I hear you ask, "will knowing your personal values enable you to make faster and more precise decisions?"

Your top three personal values are those values you try to live your life by but, consciously, you may not even be aware of what they are. Your values govern the way you treat people, how you conduct yourself and how you expect others to treat you. Mine, for instance, are honesty, trust and freedom. I try to be honest with both myself and others and I would want other people to be honest with me. Trust is an important value for me. It is important that I trust those around me but it is also important that I trust myself. I have learned to trust myself to know that, in any given situation, whatever happens to me, I'll be OK. (It took a while to learn that one!) Then, there's freedom. I love this word. Freedom to me means being able to breathe. It means being able to make my own decisions. It means being able to live my life in the way that I choose. It means choosing relationships that honour and support me as an individual. Freedom for me is important, because it gives me choices—where to be, what to do with my time and who to spend it with.

Since understanding my own top-three values, I have shaped my life around them and, because of that, I really enjoy my life. Decisions are easier to make too, as I test my options out against my personal values. For example, I'll ask myself which is the most honest choice, which option encompasses trust and which option gives me freedom. Sometimes the so-called sensible option just doesn't feel right and you might not understand why. On paper, there may be a perfectly sensible solution to a problem but, if it feels wrong, it may be because the decision clashes with your personal values.

So which values mean the most to you? Compile a list of your ten personal values that you feel are important. When you do this, don't just rush to write down as many as you can think of, or the ones your parents taught you. Choose the values that mean a lot to you, personally. This is your list, no one else's, so be completely honest.

Below is a list of words to help you. These are just suggestions and if you have others of your own, by all means use those:

Love	Excitement
Trust	Respect
Security	Humour
Integrity	Honesty
Kindness	Passion
Acceptance	Freedom
Independence	Compassion
Fairness	Happiness

Right … got your top ten? Brilliant … now the next part. If you had to choose three values for the whole world to live by, which values would you choose? (I never said this bit was easy!) These are tough choices, I know, and all your chosen values will be important to you but, if you are going to use your values as a guide, you need to come up with the three most important ones. Take your time over this and really think about it. Asking yourself these questions might help. Which of these values could I live without if I had to? Which three values do I think would make the world a better place?

So you've got your top-three personal values, what do you do with them now? Write them down and know them inside out. Remember them and use them to help make decisions with more clarity and trust.

Rachel is a perfect example of how personal values can help when making tough choices. Her top values are integrity, trust and independence. Rachel called me one day to talk through her thoughts about a job that she had been offered. She had been headhunted by a firm who were offering her a very generous financial package. At the time we spoke, Rachel was in the early days of setting up her own company. Having taken the big leap from being employed to self-employment, it would be true to say that her confidence in her ability to make her business work was being tested. Her company had been slow to start and she was not making the kind of money that she hoped she would. This job seemed to be coming at a perfect time as it offered financial stability. The only catch was that she would have to give up her own business. Rachel could see the pros and cons of this fantastic offer but, when it came to making a real choice between the two, she really hadn't got a clue what to do. So we talked the offer through using her values.

First of all, integrity. Was this offer going to be honouring Rachel's integrity? Yes, she decided it was. Then, to trust. Was this offer a true and trustworthy one? Yes, she believed it was. Then we looked at the last value, independence. Was this job offer going to give her independence? She laughed; her precise words were, "No way!" Taking this job would mean working for somebody else again, following someone else's rules and timetable. She had worked hard to branch out on her own, follow her own path and be her own boss.

With the help of her values, Rachel realised why she had been so hesitant—because, no matter how good the offer was, accepting it would have meant compromising her values. She turned down the job with a smile and a renewed conviction to make her own business work. She is finally starting to get recognition in her field and the financial rewards she deserves—a perfect example of how values can help you to de-stress and make difficult decisions with clarity.

It's a five-minute job

How to turn every day into a good day

*What annoys you every day? What really bugs you? Remember how frustrating it was when you wanted something from the bathroom cabinet and everything fell out? Don't forget how agitated you felt when you were driving and needed to wash the windscreen, only to find that you'd forgotten to fill up the water—again! How about the road tax that needs renewing and the MOT certificate you can't find? Oh, and remember the time you went to put on your favourite pair of trousers, only to find that you still hadn't repaired the zip? How frustrating is **that**! This tip is for every woman who hasn't got five minutes to do a five-minute job ...*

One frustration a day, you can cope with. Two? That might be OK, but three, four or five and you're having a really bad day. Sooner or later, you'll be snapping at the nearest person and bursting into tears if something doesn't go your way—we've all been there. But, what do you do about it? Make a list of all the things that really bug you, everything from the ring tone on your mobile or the alarm on your clock, right through to that clothes mountain building nicely in the corner of your bedroom—who *knows* what could be in there?

The best way to build up your list of annoyances is to do it over a period of days—every time you come across something that annoys you, add it to the list. The next thing to do is to work out how long each annoyance would actually take to put right. Now, you'll just have to trust me that this whole process doesn't actually take much time, just a little thought and organisation. The chances are that most of your jobs will only take five minutes. Next time you have a day off, put aside some time to fix your annoyance list, work through it and tick off the jobs as you achieve them.

Next time you want to wear those trousers, next time you want to wash your windscreen, you could be having a much better day and be feeling rather smug at the same time. The thing about five-minute jobs is that, even though you may think they're pretty insignificant and harmless, they could actually be causing you problems in all kinds of areas of your life without you even realising it.

Claire came to me because her relationship with her husband was tense and it was getting worse. It became clear that there were lots of issues to sort out but what neither one of us expected to find was that the laundry pile in the living room seemed to be causing most of the day-to-day tension.

Claire worked full time. She and her husband had five children, ranging from infant-school age to teenagers and the responsibility for the housework fell solely on Claire's shoulders.

The ironing pile would grow and grow until the weekend came, when Claire would endeavour to finish the whole lot in one hit, as well as tidy the house, act as chauffeur, friend, confidante, playmate and cook. During the week, the "mountain" was in full view, taking over part of the sofa—a constant reminder of her apparent inadequacies. She told me that her lounge was not a relaxing place. There wasn't enough room for her to cuddle up with her husband so, consequently, they sat on different sofas and communication was down to a minimum.

I asked Claire if there was a way around this. The ironing pile, she concluded, had to go. If it went, there might be a chance they could share the same sofa and, if they shared the same sofa, they might feel more relaxed together and begin to talk again. So she decided not to iron at all. Their clothes now come straight out of the tumble dryer and into the drawers, most items it seems don't even need ironing!

A huge weight had been lifted off Claire's shoulders. There was far less tension in the house and the living room was a calmer more relaxing place to be. That was over six months ago and I have since heard from Claire that there is still no ironing mountain.

Another inspirational story comes from Tanya. When Tanya came to see me she asked me to help her to manage her time more effectively. Tanya is an entrepreneur who has a booming business but she admitted she wasn't as organised as she could be. Because Tanya is self-employed, she has to log all her receipts ready to give everything to her accountant at the end of the financial year. Tanya told me just how much she hates doing this job and always puts it off until the very last possible moment. The box she stores her receipts in is usually overflowing by the time she tackles the situation. In fact, Tanya admitted to having to cross two whole days out of her work diary to put together and record all her receipts. When I asked her how much money she lost each year because of this chore, she was shocked. She had never thought about how much money she was losing. "What would happen," I suggested, "If you got rid of the receipt box altogether?" Tanya said that for starters, her shelf would look much tidier! I suggested that Tanya keep a book for her receipts to be logged in. I requested that every time she had a receipt, she logged it in the book and filed the receipt away immediately in the appropriate envelope. That way, by the time her accountant wanted to see everything, all the receipts would be logged already. Tanya agreed to put this new system into practice straight away and is working very successfully with it today. She no longer has to take two days off work to clear her backlog. She feels much more organised and in control and it only takes five minutes a day.

What have you been putting off? What would happen if all those little five-minute jobs were put right? Would you feel calmer? Less frustrated? For goodness sake, take inspiration and take the time to fix your bugbears—life is stressful enough as it is!

What's on your shopping list?

Read how to think positively and why it's so important

Is your glass half full or half empty? Do you envy those people who always seem to be so positive? Maybe you think they're just deluding themselves and that they're unrealistic? Do you never expect anything good to happen to you, just so you don't get disappointed? Then take the time to read this.

Someone once explained to me that thinking negatively is just like going to the supermarket with a list of everything you don't want! The more clients I see and friends I speak to, the more I know this to be true. Two of my friends, Teresa and Ruth, both claim to be able to save themselves a parking spot before they've reached the end of the road. Where I live, there is a very convenient road to park in, it's in the centre of town. It is notoriously difficult to park there but neither Teresa nor Ruth ever have a problem. Before they set out on their journey, they visualise the space that will be there for them. I've since done this several times and every single time, I get the space I want—right outside my favourite coffee shop.

The more I think about it, the more I realise that whatever it is you focus on, that is what ends up becoming reality. A client of mine, Terri, knows she is a negative thinker. She never enters the lottery for instance, because she knows she won't win. In her experience, trains are always delayed, she always gets stopped at red traffic lights and, you guessed it, she can never find a parking space! If you're smiling now, I'm guessing this could be you. Terri genuinely sees herself as an unlucky person and has accepted that she is someone who just seems to attract bad luck.

As far as the lottery is concerned, I'm afraid you really do have to be in it to win it but, is it really possible to influence things like trains being delayed and parking spaces being available? Can we really influence things that are seemingly so out of our control? That's what Terri asked me and, so keen was she to prove me wrong, she said she would think positively and use the visualisation techniques that both Teresa and Ruth used. What you do is this. Whatever situation you want to become a reality, you sit somewhere quiet for a minute and imagine that situation happening in your mind. Imagine your car slotting perfectly into the space you want. Imagine how pleased you'd be to see that train pulling up to the platform on time. And imagine how differently your whole day could look if those things happened.

This only takes a couple of minutes and, at this stage, I'm not asking you to believe it will happen, just visualise it happening. Then let the thought go and carry on with your day.

Terri was really astounded to find that she was beginning to influence the world around her. She started to use the positive thinking techniques I had taught her. She began expecting good things to happen and she found that she was attracting better luck. Terri's whole life was starting to change in ways she couldn't have envisaged. She went out on several shopping trips expecting to find great bargains and did so each time. She walked into meetings with her colleagues at work, expecting them to be productive and useful, and they were. Terri even bought her first lottery ticket that week and won ten pounds. The next time I saw her, she declared, "Well, you have to be in it to win it!"

It is much more important to concentrate on what you do want than what you don't. If, for instance, I asked you to avoid thinking about your next-door neighbour for a minute, I bet he or she is the first person who would come to mind. If I asked you to stop thinking about what you'd had for breakfast, I bet you couldn't help thinking about it. Your mind is a powerful piece of equipment and you control how it works. Choose what to think about and make sure you think positively.

Instead of thinking to yourself, "Don't be late, don't be late," or "Don't get it wrong, don't get it wrong," try thinking, "I'm on time," and "I'll get it right." Know what you want and concentrate on that. By compounding the negative all the time, you really do just end up with a shopping list of everything you don't want!

Get yourself sorted!

You owe good health to yourself, so make sure you're in peak condition

How is your health? OK? Not bad? Could be better? Do you worry every time you read an article on health because you know you're avoiding something? Then get the courage together to be a real woman and face your health issues head on.

Whatever you do for a living, whatever your role in this life is, if you've got a niggling concern over your health, you may not be enjoying life quite as much as you could be. When I coach a client, I look at their whole life and that includes their health. It is so much harder to enjoy life and excel at what you do, if you are constantly worried about the state of your health.

I coached Mia a few years ago because she was unhappy at work. She told me that she felt she didn't fit in.

Her colleagues would go out after work and come in the next morning full of the antics of the previous night, making her feel excluded. There was often a tense atmosphere in the office. She felt as if she had to justify her actions all the time and she put up with jibes from her colleagues about the quality and quantity of her work. So, how come Mia's colleagues were picking on her? We talked about the job itself and Mia really liked what she did. She enjoyed the customer contact and felt that she was good at her work. The only problem, she told me, was that she had been getting a lot of headaches lately. The headaches would either start in the day, making her feel so sick that she would have to go home early, or she would wake up feeling awful and not go into work at all. The result was that her colleagues often had to take her phone calls and deal with her workload as well as their own. I asked Mia to tell me how her headaches affected her. She told me that when she had them, she felt guilty for not being at work and when she didn't have them, she was always worried when the next one might come. Her social life suffered too. She often refused outings with friends to avoid the embarrassment of having to cry off sick when the time came, and at that point, she said, "It's no wonder they don't ask me out at work!"

It seems that Mia's health was making her work life ten times harder than it should have been and she was becoming unpopular in the process. Mia told me that she knew she should do something about it but worried that the frequency of her headaches might mean that it was a serious problem, so she had chosen to live with them and try to ignore them—except of course, she couldn't.

That day, Mia made a commitment to listen to her body and deal with her headaches. She decided to look into an alternative way to deal with her headaches and went to see a Kinesiologist who told her she had an allergy to certain foods. The Kinesiologist gave her a short-term eating plan avoiding those foods and Mia stuck to it.

I followed Mia's progress with coaching for three months and, in that time, her headaches virtually disappeared and she was getting on much better with her colleagues. Her social life also improved and she started going out with people from work and being involved in discussions about those "previous night antics"! Later, Mia told me that before she met me, she actually knew deep down that her headaches were the cause of the problem but felt too scared to deal with it.

So, what are you putting up with? Are you keeping your health concerns a secret in the hope they'll go away? Make the decision today to stop putting up with bad health and find out how to help your body work more effectively.

You are important to everyone in your life and you are valuable to you, so take this opportunity to be brave and do what it takes to get your health sorted out. It doesn't matter if you're trying to beat a world record or just trying to get through the day without snarling at someone, you deserve to feel the very best that you can.

Have a think for a minute. Do you always seem to complain about not feeling right? Deep down, do you know that your diet is far from healthy? Do you reach for the chocolate and coffee when you're feeling stressed, as opposed to a glass of water and some fresh air? We all eat unhealthily at times—most of us will admit to reaching for the caffeine at some point during the day—but if you're doing it consistently, your health may be suffering.

If you're really not sure what you need to be doing to address your health, who you should see or what you should be eating or avoiding, use your intuition. Ask your subconscious, "What is the best way I can help my body to be fit and well?" Then just relax and let the question go. What did you think of? Did an answer that you hadn't previously considered come into your mind? Then follow it up. I did this when I was going through a period of neck pain.

When I asked my subconscious what I needed to do, I thought of a friend of mine, Rose. I hadn't seen her for ages, so I gave her a call. It turned out that she had just done a course in Indian Head Massage and that it was very helpful for neck pain, so I had a course of six sessions with her and felt a million times better.

Make the effort to change some unhealthy habits. Take some fruit to work or swap a café latte for a mineral water. If you've got a health issue, go to your doctor and get it sorted out. The fear of not knowing what's wrong is often far worse than actually facing up to your health issues. If your doctor isn't your preferred first port of call, then find out where your nearest alternative practitioner is, as Mia did. Therapies such as Homeopathy, Kinesiology and Reflexology can help all kinds of physical as well as emotional issues.

Whatever you do today, think about your health and take some time to think about you. If you know you're lacking in energy and feel about 110 years old, now's the time to change.

Kick-start your career

Dragging yourself into work each morning? Consider this ...

Fed up with your job? Maybe you just "fell" into a career and now get more of a thrill from watching paint dry? Wonder what else is out there? Want more satisfaction from your job and your life?

Probing into the nooks and crannies of your life gives you a deeper understanding of who you are and what you want from life. Life coaching is all about changing what you don't like, in order to feel happier and more content about the way you live your life, so try this tip to kick-start your career.

For most of my clients, work is a major part of their lives. They spend a large part of their day at work and sometimes most of their free time thinking about work. Careers tend to dictate lifestyles; your place of work and the job you do accounts for such a massive part of your time, it becomes your identity and, therefore, it is so important to feel valued and satisfied with what you do.

What made you take the job you're currently doing? Have you become so caught up in office politics or day-to-day routine that you've forgotten the whole reason for doing the job you do? Try to reconnect with what attracted you to it in the first place. It could be that it wouldn't take much to put the spark back into your work. It could be that reminding yourself about what you contribute to society each day is enough to make you think differently about your occupation. Knowing your value and what you contribute to others is hugely important. If, try as you may, the spark has definitely gone and doesn't look like it's coming back, it could well be time for a change of direction.

Plenty of people take much more time and energy planning their annual holiday than they do their careers. They spend around fifty weeks of the year in a job that bores them and makes them feel undervalued, just to pay for a two week holiday every year to help them feel better about their lives! Many people tell me that they "sort of fell" into their job and now, after having worked for the same company for a long time, they've lost confidence in their ability to do anything else. Some of my clients planned their career route to the letter and have got to the top of their tree, only to find that they climbed the wrong tree in the first place and they now crave something totally different.

Whatever your circumstances, you can't change the past, so focus on the future. Have you ever asked yourself what kind of career would really excite you? There are thousands of choices in this world and people of all ages change their careers all the time. Have you ever thought about re-training? It is entirely possible.

One client of mine, Audrey, came to me because she was bored with running her holiday farm in Devon. She had ploughed an enormous amount of money and energy into a project that she was losing enthusiasm for. When I asked her what she would really love to be doing for a living, she said she had always wanted to move to Mallorca and open her own bar. At that time, her vision seemed a very long way off. However, within four months she had sold her farmhouse, put a deposit down on a bar in Mallorca and was organising her move. This is how she did it. Together we sat down and planned each step of the way. Audrey started making enquiries, getting her property valued and began information gathering. By the time it came to putting in offers for the property abroad, it felt like a very natural move. Audrey knew instinctively that she was doing the right thing.

If you weren't in the job you have now, what would you *love* to be doing? What kind of life do you want to be living? How many hours do you want and need to work each week? Could you survive on less money if it meant feeling calmer in general or more stimulated at work?

Start thinking today about your *ideal* job and take yourself mentally to a place in the future where you are in your perfect career. What kind of people are you working with? Why do you go to work every day? Are you working for yourself or someone else? Anything is possible but the idea has to be planted first. Let your imagination run wild ... I did just that.

I wrote down a list of everything I wanted to achieve in my life. In my work life, I wanted to run my own company and I wanted to be in charge of my own time and my own agenda. I wanted to make a difference to people's lives. I found that people could easily talk to me, that they asked my opinion a lot and that I enjoyed giving them the encouragement to solve their problems. I realised that the parts of my previous jobs I had enjoyed the most were getting to know my clients, talking to them and finding out how they chose to spend their time. I then worked out how much money I needed each month and how much money I'd like to earn per month (very different figures!) and slowly I had it ... my big plan. It didn't happen overnight but it did happen and I'm living it now.

Ask yourself, how do you want to be living in five years time? Start making plans.

Emotional vampires

Time to be honest: Is every friend really on your side?

Friends, family ... love them or hate them, we have a relationship with everyone we know in some form or other but not all relationships are healthy. If you're feeling drained of energy and enthusiasm, it could be to do with who you spend time with.

When I talk about relationships, I'm not just speaking about love relationships. I mean relationships in the wider sense—your relationships with your friends, your family and your work colleagues.

I have no doubt that we can all think of people in our lives who are special. The people whose company we love, who make us laugh, who take the time to really get to know us, the friends who are interested in our lives and we in theirs. These are the friends that give you an energy lift, the ones that make you feel better about everything. Then there are the other sort, the ones that seem to drain our energy. You know who they are. They're miserable, they can't help but moan about their lot in life and, every time you tell them something great about your life, they can't avoid putting a dampener on the whole thing. By the time we've finished speaking to them, we wish we'd never started the conversation in the first place! Don't get me wrong, we all have down days but there are some people who never seem to have up days, and, if you're feeling tired, bored and fed up with life, the last person you want to spend time with is another person who is tired, bored and fed up!

Think about your friends. Who energises you? Who brings you down? I'm not suggesting that you cut off all contact with people who have problems but that you think about the impact that those people and their problems have on your life.

A client of mine, Jennifer, had a friend that she had been close to since school. Jennifer's friend seemed constantly to drift from one crisis to another and had always relied on Jennifer's ongoing support and attention. Jennifer told me that she had spent hours and hours on the phone listening to her problems over the years, often making her friend feel much better by the end of the conversation. Jennifer, on the other hand, was always left feeling depressed and drained of energy. During one of our sessions, Jennifer told me that she felt she needed to put some distance between her and her friend if she was to continue with her own self-development. She was desperately trying to lose weight and get fitter but, after speaking to her negative friend, she would often find herself reaching for the biscuit tin and feeling too tired to go to the gym. Jennifer wasn't saying that her friend was solely responsible for her lack of enthusiasm for the gym, but she definitely wasn't helping.

These are difficult decisions to make and are not to be made unkindly, but who you choose to spend your time with really does affect your mood, your personality and your success. In fact, it can impact on everything to do with your life, so choose your relationships and your friends with care.

Asking yourself the following questions can help:

- What is it about this person that I like?
- What is it about this person that annoys me?
- What is it about this person that makes me want them in my life?

Maybe putting some distance between a friend or family member isn't as easy as that and you need a strategy to help you cope with their negativity. If that sounds like you, then try this exercise. When you're talking to someone and they get negative, imagine a black hole in the ground between you and them. Now imagine that their negative words and sentences are just falling down the hole. Actually see their words drain away into the ground. They can't affect or hurt you if you choose for them to disappear this way. There are many different ways of deflecting negativity but this one seems to be successful for the majority of my clients. I have also used this exercise with children who are being bullied at school and adults who feel intimidated at work or home—it does work. Use your imagination and choose not to let their words affect you.

Make a commitment to sort out the negative people in your life from your more positive friends and adapt your thinking when you have to spend time with people who drain your energy … you'll notice the difference.

Money, money, money!

Feeling the pinch? Dare to take control!

We all need it, we can't go very far without it and most of us could do with a bit more of it, but is it taking over your life? Is money starting to control you emotionally and physically? Then it's time to get it sorted.

Do you feel sick every time the credit card bill drops through the door? If you know that you're getting further and further in debt and burying your head in the sand, then refusing to look at the situation will only make you feel worse. Put the fear on hold, wise up and get a grip on your finances.

If you know you're not the best at handling your finances, that draining, nagging feeling you get every time you think about your bank statements will take its toll. It can make you feel physically ill, emotionally drained, worried and very stressed. Angela came to me because her debt problems were spiralling out of control. Her enthusiasm for life was very low and she felt so bad about letting herself get into debt that guilt, as well as her financial state, was crippling her progress. It was her desperate financial state that was at the root of her lack of self-esteem. She had lost all faith in herself and her ability to make good, trustworthy decisions regarding her future. She knew what she needed to do, but actually doing it was going to move her so far out of her comfort zone, she was convinced she'd fall at the first hurdle.

Together, we agreed that the very first step was for her to take a deep and honest look at her finances. Angela hadn't opened her bank statements for six months as she couldn't face her mounting debt, so we sat down, opened up all her financial correspondence and organised a budget for her to live on.

Angela knew roughly what was going in and out of her account but, to take control, you have to know exactly what's going on. Together, we listed all her outgoings, including the little luxuries, added it all up and adjusted the expenses until the final figure matched her earnings. Her budget was tight, but it meant she wouldn't be getting any deeper into debt.

The next thing to tackle was the feeling that she wasn't as good as everyone else. Angela saw herself as a failure and assumed that everyone else did as well. She would sometimes walk to work because she didn't have money for petrol. Angela strode down the street looking at the pavement in a bid to avoid eye contact with anyone, worrying that they would know the real reason she was walking to work. Walking to work is great exercise, though, and thousands of people do it everyday. Once Angela realised that people would only know she was in debt if she chose to tell them, she started to regain some self-esteem.

Angela very bravely took her head out of the proverbial sand and took control of her finances. Since then, she has paid off all of her debts, sold her house to downsize and can finally afford to travel and see more of the world, something she had always wanted to do. With money in the bank, her confidence is blossoming and her self-esteem literally rising by the minute.

Take a leaf out of Angela's book. If you're in debt, make a decision to educate yourself where your personal finances are concerned. Do you have any savings for a rainy day? Is your money earning the best interest it can? Have you thought about a private pension plan yet? Don't let excuses like not understanding financial jargon get between you and being financially independent and sound.

Visit a reputable independent financial adviser for advice and make sure that they talk to you in good old plain English. Don't be afraid to ask questions, even the stupid ones! If you don't understand, it's OK to say so.

Follow Angela's plan—make a list of all your outgoings each month, everything from the mortgage to your mani-cure. If you are spending more than you earn, start working out where you can cut back, do yourself a budget that fits your earnings and, the most important thing of all—stick to it! Little things can make all the difference. For instance, if you buy a magazine every day, you could be spending in excess of ten pounds a week, that's forty pounds a month. If you buy a cappuccino every lunch time, that could be another two pounds a day. Remember, every little helps.

You don't have to become a financial whiz-kid, but being in control of your finances means that you're in control of your life and your future.

Calm your environment, calm your mind!

Feeling down and miserable? It could be your laundry pile!

Do you have problems being productive? Do you find it difficult to make decisions or think clearly? Maybe you have so many things on your "to do" list, you don't know which of them to tackle first. Then this is right up your alley.

The answer could be in your environment. Your environment is anywhere that you spend time—it could be your office, your home, your car, wherever you spend most of your day. It is enormously important that you feel comfortable in your surroundings if you are going to enjoy life, stay in control and feel calm. There are enough aggravations during the course of your day that are beyond your control, so make your time more enjoyable and stress-free by adapting your environment to suit your needs and pleasures!

What do I mean? Well, do you like the way your environment is decorated? Does your office look drab and dreary? Could you do with a plant or two to brighten it up? Maybe some photos of those closest to you would make you smile in the midst of a stressful day. Maybe it's just a case of having a good old clear-up. If it's your office we're talking about, could you put a few new filing systems into place to make life easier? Would you like to move the direction of your desk and face a different way for a change? Is your chair comfortable or your computer screen user-friendly? The list is endless ... even the most subtle changes can bring a smile to your face and lift your spirits.

Sue, a client, brought a gorgeous lamp into work to sit on her desk, as she prefers its subdued light to the harsh brightness of the ceiling light. It's made a huge difference to the ambiance in her office and, for her, it's more like being at home.

Another client, Marie, called me for coaching one day when her business was struggling. She worked from home and it quickly became apparent that her environment was hugely important to her. When I asked what her office looked like, she said that although she knew where everything was, it looked completely chaotic. I asked her to describe it to me. There was a large vacuum cleaner that had taken up residence in the corner of the room, she had a few piles of old magazines on the floor, an overflowing waste-paper basket and a rather oversized piece of furniture that encroached on her space, making her office feel much smaller than it actually was. The books on the shelves were falling over and her desk really was too small. All in all, it was no wonder that her business was struggling when she was struggling to do any business in her office in the first place!

Marie agreed that her office certainly wasn't helping her to feel motivated to search for new business, so she agreed to do something about it. The following month, she proudly told me she had bought a brand-new up-to-the-minute desk and a very comfortable chair in the January sales. The hoover went, as did that huge piece of furniture and she decided to empty her waste-paper basket every day. She tidied up her environment and made it a pleasure to work in. Consequently, yep, you guessed it, her business increased.

Another story is about Megan who came to see me after her partner had just moved into her house. Megan is in her fifties and widowed with three grown-up children. She had recently invited her long-term partner to move in with her and was upset to admit that they hadn't been getting on at all well. Wondering if she had just spent too long living on her own, she was beginning to think that the new move had been a mistake. I asked Megan what exactly it was that annoyed her. It seems that Megan's house was already full to the brim with her belongings but adding her partner's worldly goods had turned the whole house upside down. Megan could no longer find anything—every surface it seemed was cluttered and there were still more boxes that her partner hadn't opened. What's more, they were stored in their bedroom, making getting into bed an obstacle course. Some of their belongings, she concluded, had to go. She spoke to her partner who agreed entirely and they spent a whole weekend going through boxes, agreeing on what to keep and what not to keep. They had so much stuff, they took two cars to the local car boot sale the following week and made over two hundred pounds. The next time we spoke, calm had been restored as had a bit of romance!

If life is getting you down, have a look around, it could well be your clutter. Change the furniture, tidy up, paint the walls, bring a plant to work or keep some relaxing lavender hand cream in your desk for when the stress gets a bit much. If you come across a fantastic photo in a magazine that really stimulates or calms you, stick it on your notice board and look at it when you're feeling frazzled. Invest a few pounds in a stretched canvas from your local art shop and paint it a colour that inspires you. You don't have to be Picasso and you don't have to spend a fortune. Act today —life doesn't have to be that tough!

Directionally challenged?

A strategy to really get you where you want to go!

Do you ever get the feeling that however hard you try to achieve something, it just slips further and further from your grasp? As a child, were you ever told to look where you were going or else you'd trip up? Well, never a truer word was spoken.

Whatever line of work you're in, whatever direction you want your life to go in, it's imperative you know what you're aiming for and head that way. Ever heard the phrase, "Don't work harder, work wiser"? Well, this tip is all about exactly that. It's about having an end goal in mind and working steadily towards that goal. It doesn't necessarily mean you have to work hard, you just have to make sure that everything you do is aligned to your end goal.

For instance, if you want to start up your own company and your day job means you work late into the evening and at weekends, finding the energy and time to start up that company of yours is going to be much harder than if you took the plunge and gave up your day job. My brother and sister-in-law, Craig and Tracey, did exactly that. They realised that, if the business they were setting up was actually going to succeed, one of them was going to have to give up work in order to spend more time on the business. Tracey's job often meant she worked long hours and she would come home too exhausted to switch on her home computer so, bravely, she handed in her notice. It meant that they had to alter their household expenses, but it was the only real way their new business was going to work and it was a risk they were prepared to take. Craig and Tracey have a very clear goal. They know where they see their business going and have even pinned up a picture above their desk of the brand-new BMW they intend to buy in a few years' time. How's that for positive thinking?

Without even realising it, Craig and Tracey are programming their subconscious minds and telling them what the future will hold. Another excellent way of making sure you keep yourself on track is to write your intentions down. I cannot overemphasise the power of writing down your plans. Just the act of putting pen to paper is powerful enough to start putting your subconscious mind to work. What I'm saying is, look in the direction you want to go and you'll stand a much better chance of getting there.

Do you actually know where you're going? Do you know where you want to be in, say, twelve months' time, two years' time? Well, if you carry on doing the same old things and thinking the same old stuff every day, you're guaranteed still to be right where you are this time next year. Now, that might be exactly what you want and, if it is, brilliant. However, if you want to be somewhere else, now is the time to start thinking about where exactly that different place is.

It's time to be specific, time to start monitoring your actions and assessing your progress properly. When I ask my clients if they know where they are going, most of them say, "Of course!" However, they don't all act as if they really do know where they're going. It's easy to get pulled off track. I'll give you an example.

I went out shopping for warm clothes last year with my husband, Nick. Even though everyone else was still in T-shirts, I was starting to feel the cold. We stood in the shop and I picked out all the gorgeous blouses and the cut-off trousers. Nick had wandered off and I was just about ready to disappear into the changing room with an armful of wonderful garments, when I got this tap on the shoulder.

"I thought you wanted warm clothes?" he asked.

"Well, I do … these will be OK, though!"

"Oh no they won't," he argued and thrust his selection of trousers and long-sleeved tops in my direction. How annoying is that! He was right and I ended up buying all the clothes he made me try on! Seduced by all the floaty, strappy numbers, I'd conveniently pushed the whole reason for my shopping trip right to the back of my mind and managed to convince myself that they'd keep me warm. My point? When you take action, make sure that it's the right sort of action. Keep a check on yourself, as Nick kept an eye on me that day. A brilliant way to keep yourself in check is to write down what you want—it's almost as if you're writing it directly on your subconscious.

The subconscious mind is a vital tool in goal setting. This is precious knowledge that I make sure every one of my clients knows about. I only wish that more people were aware of it. Your subconscious mind does thousands of jobs for you each minute, from beating your heart to producing those fabulous hormones we all love so much. It also acts like a hard drive on a computer though. It works for you and you will only get out of it the information you put into it. A couple of months ago, I was clearing out some old papers and I saw a note that I had written to myself. It was dated the day that I first saw the house I now live in and it stated my intention to buy and live in the house. At the time, I wasn't sure whether I could afford it, so it wasn't a given that it would all go through, but I'd written down my intention and let my subconscious do the rest.

I would drive up to the house and visualise removal men moving our sofas and possessions in and, yes, I did get a few strange looks, but I'm convinced it worked. When you buy a house, a lot of the paperwork and decisions are out of your control but I felt I was helping the energy move in the right direction. I got it in the end and I firmly believe that writing down what I wanted and visualising my wish led me to make the right decisions about mortgages and the other processes involved.

Put this tip into the context of your life. Write down what you want to achieve, plan how you're actually going to get there and then look right in that direction. So, are you directionally challenged?

Daydreamer

Harness the power of your subconscious to bring your dreams to life

Ever find yourself daydreaming about your ambitions actually coming true and then snap yourself out of it just in case you're tempting fate? Well, daydreaming really isn't as unproductive as you might think.

This is where you let your imagination run wild—we are off to la-la land! I have introduced you to your subconscious and now it's time to use it properly and decide exactly how life is going to be from now on.

Have a think right now about where you'd like to be this time next year. Got a picture in your mind? Good. Go somewhere quiet and close your eyes. Imagine that you are already at that point in time—maybe you got a promotion at work, maybe you're earning more money, perhaps you've found your soul mate or maybe you gave up your office job and are now a safari tour guide in Africa. How does it feel to be doing what you're doing? What are you wearing? What are you saying? Who are you with? It is important that you really feel this picture, make it as real as you can. Then, let the image go and open your eyes. You have now planted a very real and firm idea in the depths of your subconscious. It will work for you from now on, and what is more, it will work to make sure that it becomes reality. You can help this process by writing down every-thing you saw in your daydream—remember the power of writing down your thoughts is real and should not be underestimated.

If you want to be even more specific, plan your objective precisely in your daydream and write down each step. Do this by picturing your end goal. Imagine you are already there and imagine you are being interviewed on your success. Now imagine the interviewer asks, "What was the very first thing you did to get you closer to your dream?" Imagine what your answer would be and then write it down. Now imagine what you did next, then write that down too. Write down each person you spoke to, every place you went for inspiration or advice. Did you have to re-train to do your current job and how did you find out about the training course you eventually went on? If you are serious about making your dreams a reality, you need to be as precise and specific as you possibly can. Take time to do this— your future is worth investing some time and energy in.

I know this sounds incredibly simple, but by letting your subconscious in on your ambitions, it can be making progress while your conscious mind is doing other things. You know when you read through a magazine and you read a headline? Often that headline is taken from a sentence in the main body of the article. Do you find that your eye is automatically drawn to that sentence in smaller print in the middle of the article, surrounded by a whole load of other text? Ever wondered why your eye was drawn to that point? Well, your subconscious scanned the article very quickly and took your conscious mind directly to something it recognised. If it can do that, imagine what it can do if, for instance, you are looking for a specific solic-itor; one, for, example who specialises in buying property abroad. If you've daydreamed about finding that lawyer, visualised seeing the ad in the paper, imagined making the phone call and finding out everything you need to know, your subconscious will scan what you look at, what you read and what you hear, bringing your attention straight to the information you need.

As a result, you will start to notice all the things that you need in order to put your plan into practice. Use this wisely and daydream, daydream, daydream!

How do you feel today?

Alter your mood, just because you feel like it!

Wouldn't it be great to wake up every morning feeling fabulous, gorgeous and positive? Well, maybe that feeling is not a million miles away after all. How did you feel when you woke up today? Worried? Stressed? Tired? Then try this idea.

Some days, it seems like we just wake up in a bad mood. Sometimes, we get out of bed on the wrong side and the whole day goes pear shaped. Our hair doesn't go right, we're late for work, the car needs petrol, the coffee spills over the desk and we snap at our colleagues. Some days may just as well be written off.

It doesn't have to be like that though. How would you *like* to wake up feeling? Did you know that it is entirely possible to turn a potentially bad day into a good one, just by persuading yourself that it *will* be good? When you wake up tomorrow, when you're still in that drowsy, "not quite with it" stage, instead of listing everything that needs to be done that day, ask yourself this question—"How do I want to feel today?" Maybe you have a two-year-old child who is testing your patience and you need to be calm. Maybe a colleague at work is feeling negative at the moment and you need to be the positive one or maybe you just want to feel more in control?

My client, Michelle, is the perfect example of how you can literally change your mood and habits overnight. Michelle came to me initially because she wanted a rela-tionship. A successful PA with a demanding job, there had been little time for romance and she was feeling completely fed up with her own company. During her first session, I was hearing a lot about how miserable and grumpy she was, especially first thing in the morning and even more so on the days when the train to work was delayed. If her journey didn't go well, as far as she was concerned, her whole day was ruined. Michelle knew she was snapping at people who didn't deserve it and was sarcastic to others who were just trying to be pleasant. She realised that she had to deal with her bad moods and be more patient with everyone if she was going to attract a date.

When I asked Michelle to describe herself, she told me she was unhappy, intolerant and ugly. Not a great combination if you want a love life! I asked Michelle to come up with three new words, the exact opposite of those she had just told me, and she came up with a much better bunch— Happy, Tolerant and Gorgeous! Powerful words for a girl that meant business. I asked Michelle to repeat those words to herself ten times in the morning just as she was waking up, ten times in the evening just before she went to sleep and at any other time during the day when she felt she needed a reminder.

It has to be said that despite being somewhat unsure of the potential success of this exercise, Michelle gave it her best shot and worked very hard at it. First thing in the morning, every morning and whenever she felt herself get angry or short with someone she would repeat Happy, Tolerant, Gorgeous. Michelle really impressed me. Not only was she calmer the next time I spoke to her but she was happier, liked herself more and was much more tolerant at work. She no longer got annoyed or angry when the train was late. In fact, she even laughed at everyone around her when they got stressed. She did fantastically well and she got in touch with me just a few weeks ago. While on holiday in New Zealand, she met her perfect man. She's very much in love and is moving to the other side of the world to be with him. Michelle firmly believes that if she had met her boyfriend before she started thinking differently about herself, she wouldn't have been in the right frame of mind to cultivate a relationship with him and they may never have got together.

Follow Michelle's lead. Take a deep breath and literally breathe in that feeling—just take a few moments to *be* that feeling—exhale and smile. Whenever the day starts to go downhill, just remember how you wanted to feel at the beginning of the day and catch that feeling again—it really does work but don't take my word for it, try it and see.

Go on, flex those muscles!

Easy, tiger—I mean, confidence muscles! Boost your confidence, without Lycra!

Do you clam up and become a gibbering wreck when someone you like walks into the room? Does speaking at meetings scare the hell out of you? Do you look at everyone else and marvel at how confident and capable they are? Then you need to get to the gym ... the confidence gym.

Relax, ladies, you don't need to get your Lycra out to show off these muscles! Building your confidence is just like building up your muscles at the gym—the more you flex your confidence muscles, the stronger they get. So what do your confidence muscles look like?

First of all, it is important for you to define the word "confidence". Confidence means different things to different people. It can be as ambiguous as the word "happy". My dog wants to be happy but a bowl of dog food and a walk will do the trick—my guess is that you'll need more than that. So take a few minutes to answer the following questions:

- What exactly does the word "confidence" mean to you?
- What does a confident person look like?
- How do they act?
- How do they dress?
- What sort of things do they say?
- How do confident people hold themselves?

Everyone's version of "confident" will be different. What is it that *you* specifically need to do in order to feel more confident about yourself?

With these questions in mind, take a pen and paper and write down ten things that would need to happen for your confidence in yourself to bloom. It could be anything from learning to drive to wearing red lipstick—it doesn't matter what you write as long as it is important to you.

The next step is to decide which of those two ideas you could actually put into practice today. Please note the word "you" here. Unfortunately, no matter what other people do, they will never be able to boost your confidence for you. So when you answer these questions, make sure that you work out exactly what you need to do in order to enhance your confidence muscles, then be bold and go do it.

My client, Ruth, was brave enough to put her plan into action, with glittering results. When I first met Ruth, she hid behind her long hair. She wore men's jumpers, at her own admission, "To hide my horrible figure," and she admitted she rarely looked people in the eye when she spoke to them because she didn't want to be seen. What I saw, though, was a very attractive woman. Ruth was funny— she made me laugh, had a cracking sense of humour and a great smile. We spoke about what confidence meant to her. I asked her to close her eyes for a few minutes and picture herself looking fabulously confident. This is what she saw—Ruth walking down the High Street where she lived, wearing smart but comfortable clothes. She visu- alised herself with a tan, blonde streaks in her hair, smiling and making eye contact with people who looked at her. As you can imagine, she had pictured an image that was a million miles away from the way she looked that day. I asked her to put two of those things into practice that very week. She chose from her list and promised to make eye contact with the very next person she bought something from and she said she would smile when she did it.

Ruth came back to me one month later and, I have to say, the transformation astonished me. Ruth had a tan (because after our session, she had gone out, booked and been on a week's holiday) and she was wearing women's clothes that fitted perfectly and made her look great. She had a different hairstyle, which framed her face, and she had been making regular eye contact with the people she spoke to. Ruth felt amazing and looked it, too.

That was three years ago. I caught up with her recently and was speechless when I opened the door to her. I would not have recognised her had I seen her in the street. Ruth had lost four stone, wears gorgeous trendy clothes and has a fabulous choppy blonde hair cut. She goes to the gym three times a week, is divorcing her husband amicably and considering a move to the other side of the country. She looks ten years younger than she did when I was coaching her. She's an amazing woman who simply decided that enough was enough and she had to change.

Feeling more confident isn't just about looking the part —it goes much deeper. If you know you look good, though, it certainly goes a long way towards making you feel great on the inside too. A friend of mine, Fiona, told me that she once had a dress that, even years later, she still remembers feeling fantastic in. She knew she looked good whenever she went out in it and she remembers how great things always used to happen to her in that dress. I remember, too, a time when I went to a party with my friend, Emma. We took the train up to London after she had just come back from a holiday where she'd acquired a golden tan and natural blonde highlights from the sun. She wore a cheeky, short, lime-green dress and looked just brilliant. Confidence radiated from her and we both had a fantastic time.

What do you need to do to feel more confident? It's important to feel good about yourself. When you glow with confidence, imagine what a beneficial effect that has on your children and on the friends and family around you. Make sure you give your confidence muscles a work-out today.

Enjoying the ride

If you're never satisfied with life, this strategy will fill you with pride

Are you never completely happy with your lot in life? Do you have difficulty concentrating on the job in hand because your mind is already two paces ahead? Maybe you're so focused on attaining your dream that you're forgetting about the here and now?

I'm always talking to my clients about their future—what they want from it, where their life is going and what sort of life they're aiming for, even if it's just getting the kids to bed earlier so they can have a bath on their own. It's just as important though to remember the here and now. Life is about balance and time seems to pass so quickly that sometimes it's easy to miss the day-to-day things that can bring so much pleasure.

Enjoying the ride is about taking stock, looking around at the things you've achieved so far and the people you have in your life. It's not about worrying about events that haven't happened yet, it's about being proud of what you already have and the person you are at this very moment.

Your capacity to achieve great things is massive but don't forget that the "now" was yesterday's "future". If you never take the time to appreciate the now, you'll always be chasing the future and that's just a dream. Don't get me wrong—without dreams, man would never have gone to the moon and the light bulb may never have been invented, but do spend some time in the here and now, too. Otherwise, by the time you've reached your destination, you'll have missed the journey and it's the journey where you did all your growing.

I came to realise just how important the here and now was, when a friend of mine, Stavros, died very suddenly. Stavros was one of the kindest men I have ever met. A talented dancer and choreographer, he was always full of energy. He organised the venues for our shows in Greece. He also made all our costumes and worked with us to put on the most amazing shows. He looked out for us and even cooked for us most days. Ten dancers, including me, travelled by train up to Larissa from Athens. We were to work in a fabulous open air venue for the summer. Stavros was so excited, he had spent months organising everything, creating brand-new costumes for everyone and new songs and dances for us to perform. He had choreographed, sewed and stayed awake most of the night making sure it was all perfect. Then, on the way to our new venue, he was involved in a major collision, which killed both him and his best friend. We were all waiting at the hotel for them, joking about how they had probably stopped off for something to eat but, of course, the jokes stopped when we got the phone call. I had never ever been in a situation like that before. It was so sudden and desperately sad, but at least Stavros had lived in the moment and that was a great lesson I learned from him.

Living in the moment is about appreciating the things and the people we have around us right now. Look around you and really see the things that make your life special— children growing up, nieces and nephews to adore, cats and dogs that are always pleased to see you and the friends you love to laugh with. When I was a teenager, we used to spend part of Christmas (usually Boxing Day) with family. When all the cousins and aunts and uncles got together there were quite a few of us! Every year, it was held at my Auntie Pam's house, and each year, we were given a job to do to help prepare the evening buffet. Most years, Nan got to prepare the prawns. I will never forget my Uncle Mike signalling to me to watch my nan. He had a big grin on his face and we secretly watched as Nan peeled the prawns. She'd peel one or two that went in the bowl and another that went very quickly into her mouth, hoping that no one would notice. My Uncle Mike said, "You'll remember this!" and I have to this day. It still brings a smile to my face. It's these kinds of magic memories I'm talking about, seeing what's right in front of you and really enjoying it.

Looking to the future is excellent and, if we don't plan where we're going, we stand a big chance of not getting there but, while you strive for a future with more clarity, less stress and more fun, don't forget to enjoy each day as well.

If you lived in the moment more, what would you be doing differently? Not worrying as much? Enjoying your weekend more? Being a bit more patient with loved ones?

What can you do to really "enjoy the journey"? It might be something simple like enjoying your food more, instead of gulping it down as quickly as possible. It might be giving a friend an extra five minutes of your time. Live in the moment and enjoy the life you live now.

The High/Low game

Having trouble communicating? From difficult teenagers to strained relationships, find out more about your friends and family with this great game

Do you find it hard to communicate with loved ones? Do you wish you had a better understanding of what goes on in the lives and minds of your friends and family? This could be your answer ...

When there's precious little time to spare and so many people to share it with, it can be easy to miss what's going on in someone else's world. This tip is not complicated—in fact, it's very simple. It promotes communication and opens up all kinds of channels to build relationships. It's called the High/Low game. You can play it with your partner, your children, friends, colleagues, in fact anyone you spend time with and want to communicate better with.

The High/Low game builds bridges where needed, helps you to connect with someone on a deeper level, promotes your understanding of how your loved one sees his or her own world and ultimately brings people closer together.

Here's how it works. When you get home or the children run in from school, whatever you're doing, make time during the evening to sit down, turn the television off and talk. Your opening line is, "What was your high today and what was your low?" Your high might be the feeling you got when you did a job really well at work and your boss finally noticed. Your low could have been not having anyone to talk to at lunch time. This is more than just asking how someone's day went—they can't get away with a simple "fine" or "OK"—you are asking about how they felt during the day. You're asking about the best thing that happened and the worst thing that happened and only by asking them to be this specific, will you learn something about your loved ones' world that you may not otherwise have known. It brings up topics that wouldn't normally have been discussed. It gives you the opportunity to understand how the other person ticks or why, for instance, they might be in a bad mood.

Open up your conversation, listen to someone else's high and low—and I do mean listen. Don't interrupt until they've finished—that's *the* most important part of this game. Stop what you're doing, look at them when they're speaking to you and keep quiet until they've finished, then you can have your say!

Seize the moment, girls!

Great inspiration—take advantage of opportunities

Do you dismiss opportunities that are offered on a plate and then kick yourself because you didn't speak up? Take inspiration from this tip and "do a Holly"!

The inspiration for this tip comes from a tenacious little dog called Holly. I was recently invited to be a judge at the Wag and Bone Dog Show at Ascot. Oh yes, we life coaches get to do all kinds of interesting things on our weekends off.

My job was to judge the Loveable Rogue competition. Just before the competition, I bought a cuddly toy and had it with me in a plastic bag when I was judging. A gorgeous dog named Holly took absolutely no notice of me when I went over to make a fuss of her and ask her owner why she should be considered a loveable rogue. Little Holly was determined to show me instead and went straight for the toy, and she wasn't going to give it up easily. She tugged at it and pulled at it with great determination—she really wanted it and it took a good few minutes before her owner persuaded her that the toy wasn't hers to take.

Far from being annoyed at my soggy cuddly toy, however, I couldn't help being mightily impressed by her determination to get what she wanted—she was definitely a girl with a mission and it's that tenacity that I help my clients to cultivate. Little Holly saw what she wanted and went for it.

The moral of this story, of course, is "seize the moment"! Sometimes it seems as if opportunities just present themselves to us for no apparent reason. Maybe it's coincidence, good luck, being in the right place at the right time, fate, whatever you want to call it. It does happen and when it does, you want to know that you'll have the confidence to say "yes".

Just occasionally, people do kind things for others. They offer perfectly respectable and above-board opportunities when they see potential in a person. It has been known for people to offer chances for others to shine and give them the occasion to prove themselves, just because they can.

Some of my more positive friends and clients tell me how they are often offered fantastic opportunities, such as chances to meet people and do things they would never otherwise have done. Negative people, on the other hand, either don't seem to see opportunities that are presented to them or are too sceptical and afraid to take the chance, so they pass them up. If someone is prepared to give you a break and you trust that person, listen to your intuition and, if it doesn't alert you, grasp the opportunity with both hands. Have a little faith in yourself and shine.

Knowing that you'll be good enough is massively important and it could mean that you open up all kind of follow-up possibilities for yourself.

Are there opportunities that you could have taken? Do you have any at the moment and are you really taking advantage of them? Sometimes, the chance to do things, say things or learn things is just handed to us but, if we're too shy to take it and don't have the confidence to say "yes", we really could be missing out. So, do a Holly, take the opportunity and seize the moment!

(If you're wondering by the way, yes, Holly did win First prize for the most loveable rogue.)

All work and no play ...

Accused of being serious all the time?
Maybe they're right, let
your hair down!

Oh, for goodness sake, have fun! Do you get so wrapped up in the business of paying bills, meeting deadlines, being responsible and keeping everything and everyone together that you wind up feeling dull, uninteresting and lifeless? Then you need some good old-fashioned fun.

This tip involves nothing more than laughing like you haven't laughed in ages!

Most of the women I talk to each week run not only their own lives, but the lives of their children, their partners as well as their bosses. We just can't help ourselves. We list all our weekend jobs and can't say "no" to running errands, doing favours and helping other people out. We do all this in between our own tasks—going to the bank, washing, ironing, cleaning and making sure the children finish their homework. The list is never-ending. All too often, the weekend has passed before we even realised it had arrived.

Everyone else seems rested, yet we return to work on Monday morning exhausted—so next weekend, make it different and have some fun.

Say "no" to errands, tell those closest to you that you've made plans, make a decision to put yourself first and ask yourself how you'd really like to spend your weekend.

Years ago when we were both feeling a bit frazzled, my friend Emma and I booked two theatre trips in one week. One was to see Ben Elton and the other to see Lenny Henry. It was a bit extravagant and ever so slightly exhausting but we had such a ball. I have never laughed so much in one week. It was an absolutely brilliant lift and the best happiness therapy.

Would you like to run off to the seaside for two days? Perhaps you'd just like to sit in the paddling pool on a hot summer's day with the children and play. Maybe you'd love to get together with the girls, go shopping, have lunch out and round the evening off eating popcorn and pretending not to cry at a soppy film? Perhaps you'd love to go to a theme park for the day and try out all the rides. Whatever you choose to do, the housework will wait. Have fun and enjoy yourself—Monday mornings will seem *so* much more appealing!

Are you sitting just a little too comfortably?

Bored with life or afraid to try new things? Be inspired …

Are you stuck in a rut? Do you feel like all the excitement has been drained out of your life? Have you lost the confidence you once had? Then think about this ...

Every one of us has a comfort zone. Your comfort zone is the life you live now. It's the job you have, the routine you've built for yourself, the friends you spend time with, the hobbies you enjoy, the holidays you go on and the qualifications you hold. Your comfort zone is all the things in your life that make "you" feel like "you". In short, it's your safety net. You may not be a rocket scientist or a brain surgeon but you know your limitations, right? You know what you're good at and what you're not. Maybe you're sitting quite comfortably, thank you! But are you sitting just a little too comfortably?

Do you ever stretch your comfort zone? The comfort zone you have built for yourself might feel safe but it may not be a space in which you can blossom and grow. Maybe secretly you know that you are hindering your personal growth because you're too scared to stretch those comfortable boundaries?

When you left primary school, you stretched your comfort zone. When you left senior school, you stretched your comfort zone. When you left home for the first time, you stretched your comfort zone. But are you still stretching? When was the last time you did something that frightened or challenged you? Stretching your comfort zone can be doing anything from going for a promotion or giving yourself the chance to do something you'd previously considered impossible. It could mean going somewhere completely different for a holiday, trying to learn a new language or taking up an exhilarating new hobby. Imagine, for instance, what your children or friends might say if you took up clay pigeon shooting or flying lessons. Imagine how proud they would be. Have you ever considered being a Special in the police force? What about voluntary work? What about doing something courageous for charity? Now, jumping out of an aeroplane may not be your "thing" but what would you love to do?

One of my clients, Mary, came to see me exactly one year into her retirement. Mary had spent a long time anticipating her retirement years, only to find that she was bored stiff. Her two daughters had families of their own and her former work colleagues no longer invited her out. As a result, her social life had faded away and she was desperate not to fade away, too. Mary told me she had always had such a busy life surrounded by people and things to do but now, living on her own, she was losing her sparkle and was desperate to relight it again. I asked Mary what she did before her family and busy career came along and one of the things she had enjoyed was painting. In fact, she told me, she had been quite good. Despite the fact that Mary hadn't picked up a paintbrush for more than forty years, her face lit up. She now attends her local art group regularly and holds annual exhibitions. She has been featured in local papers several times and is quite the social diva!

If you've stopped stretching, you could be doing yourself out of living a life that *completely* fulfils your dreams. You could be missing out on a diva's opportunities, memories to smile at or even the chance to change your whole life.

Stretching your comfort zone is not about quitting your career tomorrow or walking out of your life today. It's about looking at life from a different perspective and asking yourself if it fulfils you and makes you feel proud of where you are and who you are. This is a rare opportunity for you to question (if you dare) the way you live your life and an opportunity to consider living it in a different way and trying something new.

If you've landed the job of your dreams—great! If you've got an amazing relationship that allows you to grow— fantastic! But if you haven't? Dare to imagine for a minute, how your life might be if you did have those things. What would you be doing? What would you look like? How would you be feeling?

The feeling of actually doing something that others just talk about is truly amazing. You'll grow in stature, you'll develop into a stronger human being, and you'll develop a sense of confidence in yourself that you previously envied in others. So ... are you sitting just a little too comfortably?

Say what you mean

A guide to getting on better with people

Are there people in your life that you just don't understand? Do they seem to say one thing then do the exact opposite? Frustrating as this is, you could be totally missing each other's point. This might help.

Say exactly what you mean and understand exactly what someone else means ... confused? I'll explain.

Everyone has different meanings and interpretations for the same word. For instance, if you ask one person to describe a "confident" woman, they might describe someone in a bar laughing and joking with a complete stranger, whereas someone else may well view that person as being flirtatious. Their interpretation of a "confident" woman might be someone quietly enjoying a drink on their own. It's all too easy to misunderstand someone by assuming that their version of the words we use in everyday language are the same as yours—every one of us is different and we all think differently.

Maybe you aren't getting along with a colleague or partner, maybe you work really hard to make your boss happy, only to find that you've done it wrong (again!) or maybe you have to work with someone that you just don't seem to get on with. When you next speak to them, check that their understanding and your understanding of certain words or phrases are the same.

I recently coached Serena, who was going through a difficult patch in her marriage. When I spoke to her, her main gripe about her husband was that she felt he had never provided for her and the children. The word "provide" kept coming up in their conversations and causing arguments with her husband. He claimed that he had always provided the very best he could for his family. I asked Serena to explain exactly what the word "provide" meant to her. She told me that her husband had never earned enough money to take the children on exotic holidays or buy them the latest clothes. She had always had to work hard to contribute to the household expenses and she was tired of not being "provided" for, by which, of course, she meant financially. I asked her to talk to her husband about his version of the word "provide", so she did. Not surprisingly, his version was completely different. He saw himself as a provider because of his ability to love his family. He had always been a "hands-on" father. He had been there to put on plasters and to wipe away tears. In fact, Serena had often remarked on just how good he had been in that respect. They had been arguing and completely missing each other's point of view because they had never sat down and each asked what the other meant.

Another client of mine, Samantha, was the managing director of a company with a busy schedule that allowed no margin for error. She came to me because her workload was becoming increasingly heavy and she was making costly mistakes. During the course of our first session, it became clear that Samantha didn't get on with her PA. It seemed that she was actually doing a lot of her PA's tasks because she couldn't rely on her assistant to take on the responsibility of her role. In the short time the PA had worked for Samantha, she had already had to speak to her on several occasions about her inability to do what was expected of her. So I asked Samantha exactly what she meant by that. She told me that she expected her PA to be her eyes and ears as she was under so much pressure. She needed her to take routine calls and make day-to-day decisions on her behalf, things that her assistant just wasn't doing. I asked Samantha if she thought her PA really understood what was needed and whether she knew exactly what was meant by "taking responsibility for her role". I suggested she sit down with her and explain exactly what it was she wanted her to do and to assure her that she felt confident she could do it.

I met Samantha a month later and discovered that their whole relationship had changed. They were getting on really well and her PA was so efficient that Samantha found the capacity to take on three more accounts. Samantha admitted that previously she had been snappy with her, often in front of other directors, which had contributed to her PA's inability to be effective because her confidence had been so undermined.

If you're not "getting" someone, ask them specifically what they mean—you might just find the key to a happier relationship.

Clear your wardrobe, clear your mind

Feeling frumpy? The answer could be in your underwear drawer!

Are you fed up with your clothes? Do you feel frumpy compared to everyone else? Well, do something about it and clear out your wardrobe. "How can that possibly be a life coaching tip?" I hear you ask. Oh, you'd be surprised ...

When I say clear out your wardrobe, I mean take a good and objective look at all your clothes (yes, including the depths of the dreaded underwear drawer!). Have some of your clothes passed their best-by date? Do they still even fit you properly? Have you been meaning to send them to the dry cleaners? Do you need to get them altered? Are they looking tired and faded? Do you still feel good when you wear them?

Do something positive and either get them sorted out or admit that they should no longer take up precious space in your wardrobe. Having a good clear out is enormously therapeutic and actually helps to relieve stress. When you de-clutter your personal space, you're also de-cluttering your mind, leaving space and room for new and exciting things to enter your life. Filling bags full of clothes for charity shops and moving forward with your life brings a huge sense of satisfaction. You'll feel fantastic when you next open your wardrobe door and the thought of some new clothes to replace the old ones will bring a smile to any girl's face.

When you're going through your clothes, ask yourself a few questions and be brutally honest. Ask yourself, "Have I worn this in the last year?" "Do I feel comfortable wearing this?" "Is this still in fashion?" If you're keeping any clothes because someone bought them for you or because they were expensive at the time, this is the perfect time to give them away. If there's anything you've never liked, chuck it out today! By being ruthless and treating yourself to a few new items for work and some brand-new gorgeous lingerie, you'll feel good, your spirits will lift and you'll look great.

You've already read about Michelle and her "Happy, Tolerant, Gorgeous" motto. When Michelle came to me, the last thing she expected me to ask her about was the state of her underwear drawer! Michelle needed to look gorgeous as well as feel it, so while her new-found motto was busy imprinting the "gorgeous" message on her sub-conscious, I asked her to get to work on her underwear drawer. Michelle's homework for that week was to go on a shopping spree for knickers! Having cleared out all her old stuff and refilled her drawers with fabulous new lingerie, Michelle felt great. Just to be able to feel delicious, sexy lingerie under your clothes is enough to boost any girl's self-esteem.

It's probably not just clothes in your wardrobe, though— what else is lurking at the back there? Old photos? Unused Christmas presents? The odd sock, whose partner left home some time ago? When I ask my clients to go through their wardrobes, they find the most surprising things.

Jayne came to see me because of the clutter building up around her home. She was constantly losing things, felt really disorganised and her clothes mountains were getting out of control. We started in the bedroom as this was the most disorganised place in Jayne's house. At the bottom of Jayne's wardrobe was a box of photos and belongings from a past relationship. It was clearly a relationship that still upset Jayne a lot. Going through the cupboard we discovered other reminders—jumpers they had shared and the dress she had worn on their first date. What was happening was that every time Jayne opened her wardrobe she saw the things that reminded her of her past relationship. As well as cluttering up her wardrobe, these reminders were also acting as an obstacle for anyone new to come into her life and this was borne out by the fact that Jayne hadn't had another boyfriend since that relationship had ended eight years ago. She was not only holding on to the belongings associated with that time but also the feelings, so she agreed to let them go.

Take this opportunity to make sure that everything you own is a pleasure to wear. Make sure that you feel really good in your clothes. As a general rule, if you didn't wear it last year, you won't wear it this year. If you use excuses like, "it was a bargain" or "I just need some shoes to go with them", get yourself in check. Don't keep things just because they were a bargain—things are only ever a bargain if you've got a lot of wear out of them and, if they've still got the price tag on, you were done, so throw them out!

Get your wardrobe sorted out, use clear storage boxes so you know what's inside, separate your winter and summer clothes to make more space in your wardrobe and put up some new shelving to make things easier to reach. As for those shoes buried at the bottom, well, sort through those too, Imelda Marcos! Anywhere there's a recycling bank, there is usually a shoe bank. Do make sure you throw them away in pairs—one shoe isn't good to anyone! Old, misshapen or worn shoes should go, as well as the ones that hurt your feet. Be bold and be brave. If you look and feel great, your self-esteem will fly—it works a treat!

Are you really listening?

Improve your relationships on all levels and you don't have to say a word

Are you really listening? Do you know deep down that you don't really listen to your partner or family as you should? Maybe you're the one they're deaf to and you feel let down by those around you? This one is just for you ...

Listening is a huge part of communication and if you really listen to the people around you, you will improve and strengthen your relationships.

When you talk to your children, your partner, your work colleagues or your parents, are you really giving them all of your attention and making them feel like the most important people in the room? It is essential that you really hear what people tell you. They give you their version of how they see the world and how events affect them. Everyone's viewpoint is a valid one, even if it differs from your own, and you never know what you might learn if you really pay attention. Here's a quick checklist to see if you're really listening:

- You are *not* listening to someone when you interrupt their sentences and finish them;
- You are *not* listening to someone when you are preparing your side of the argument while they are still speaking;
- If you find your mind wandering on to your list of "to do" jobs, then you are *definitely* not listening; and, oh yes …
- If you are using hand signals to pass on a message to someone else whilst on the phone, the person on the other end of the phone will know!

We have all been guilty of this at some point, but it is time to stop. When you feel someone is really listening to you, you feel valued, your self-esteem rises and, even if they don't agree with you, you know that they have respected your point of view. So, do the same for others, make time and listen to them.

A fellow coach and great friend of mine, Suzanne, was really surprised to discover that she hadn't been listening to her husband as well as she thought she had. After beginning her coaching course some years ago, she was dying to try out her new improved listening skills with someone, so she tried them out on her husband. In her words, she started "shutting her mouth"! Suzanne's husband is a slow speaker, unlike Suzanne who speaks very quickly. Suzanne started to become aware of how she desperately wanted to finish off his sentences, something that she had always done, without even realising it. The more she listened, the more he talked, and it wasn't until about one month later, he said, "You talk to me differently." What an amazing thing to say! In actual fact, she hadn't been talking to him any differently, she had been listening to him a whole lot more!

It's so easy to put words into other people's mouths, but when we do this, we take away their sense of expression. When my clients first start to try this, they feel uncomfortable with the silent pauses that sometimes arise. Silence is very necessary though, and it doesn't mean that communication stops just because there isn't a stream of words. People sometimes need silences to make sure they express themselves in exactly the way they want. Even after someone has finished speaking, if we remain silent for a few seconds, chances are they'll carry on and you'll learn even more about them.

Many of my clients tell me that's partly why they feel their coaching sessions are so beneficial. They say it's because someone is really listening to what they're saying. Do your friends, family and colleagues listen to you? Try telling them about this tip and agree to start listening to each other properly. Every single time I have made a client aware of their own listening skills, their relationships improve and, quite often, they feel more heard as well. People can discover the most amazing new things about people they've known for years. When you really listen, you give someone the space to express themselves, to form an opinion of their own and tell you how they really feel.

So, keep quiet until the person has finished their sentence, formulate your response only when they have finished speaking. Look at them when they are speaking to you, concentrate on what they are saying and see what happens.

Be inspirational!

Getting that invisible feeling?
Read this one

Feeling drained of energy? Feeling worthless, undervalued and invisible? Well, you wouldn't be the first woman in history to feel like that but wouldn't it be good if you were the last ... read this.

Know your value, inspire and be inspired. No matter who you are, what you do, whatever your background or how old you are, you are always capable of being an inspiration to someone else.

At some time in your life, whether you realise it or not, you will have touched someone and moved that person enough to want to better themselves. You may even have given them the courage to get through the day without even knowing it. You will have said something that pushed someone else just that little bit harder, which meant that they felt they were able to accomplish and achieve something difficult. Inspiring people gives rewards beyond measure. That's why I do the job I do, because I get to see people grow and blossom. When I've motivated someone to make a move they considered scary or impossible and they succeed at it, it improves the quality of my day, too. I see potential in my clients that they may not appreciate is there, and it is my job as their coach to help them realise their ability to be the wonderful person I can see.

You don't have to be a coach to do this, though. All you have to do is see potential in other people and encourage them to take those first steps. You probably inspire other people without even knowing it and, in fact, the true and magic quality of inspiring someone is that you don't always know when or how it happened. It is not about boasting what a good friend you are or pushing someone to do something that they really cannot achieve or that they really don't want to achieve. Being inspirational often comes in sentences of very few words. It's in those words that a seed can be planted in someone else's subconscious and, once it's planted, it grows. They hear what you say, they mull it over and, if they were the right words, they make their move, act and achieve.

Being inspirational is like giving someone a spark to be able to light a fire of their own. Sometimes, it's the small things that inspire others. Perhaps you're going through a difficult patch and it's as much as you can do to get through the day and still smile at the end of it, but the chances are, someone has noticed how well you deal with certain situations and has been inspired by you.

A friend of mine organised her wedding to her fiancé of nine years. Just weeks after tying the knot, she discovered he had been having an affair. From that moment onwards, her life was turned upside down and she had to find a strength of character she wasn't sure she had. She went through a stressful divorce and had to fight to keep the flat they once shared. She also had to learn to live on her own for the first time, to deal with devastating bouts of loneliness, depression and debt before slowly pulling herself up and making it through to the other side. My friend had to learn from scratch how to trust her own decisions again. It's stories like this that inspire others to find the strength to fight their own battles and know that if you can do it, so can they. My friend is far too modest to label herself an inspiration but I think she is … so I'll do it for her … you know who you are—well done, girl!

Another great friend of mine, Rebecca, was inspired last year when she went to a concert. There were a group of deaf children signing to a song. Rebecca felt so inspired by these brilliant children that she learnt to sign herself and now teaches deaf children with learning difficulties.

Has anyone ever told you that you've been their inspiration? Has anyone ever commented on how well they think you deal with adversity? Next time they do, take pride, know your value and be inspired.

Do you have a mind to be rich?

Want to improve your earning power? Let your subconscious do the hard work, not you!

Have you ever wondered why some people always seem to fall on their feet where money is concerned? Do you work hard but all your efforts never seem to make any difference to your bank balance? Do you think it unfair that some people just get lucky? Well, the truth is, your attitude could well be sabotaging your own success.

What are your thoughts and beliefs concerning money? Are you secretly jealous of other people's good fortune? Do you expect money to be hard to come by? Maybe you're of the opinion that money is at the root of all evil?

As you've already read, every thought you have gets locked into your subconscious. By harbouring negative thoughts concerning money and by being jealous of others' wealth, you are effectively training your subconscious to believe that it is wrong to have abundance—so why on earth would you expect your subconscious to lead you to abundance when it's so wrong? You are training it to believe that not only is it wrong to have a stronger earning power but that you aren't worthy of earning more anyway! You now know that your subconscious mind believes every word you say and takes what you say literally, so watch your thoughts, they really are very powerful.

Refine your internal dialogue, review your beliefs and that could all change. Think positively about money. Be pleased for friends or colleagues that are doing well—wish them every success and you'll be on the right road to start retraining your subconscious. Expect success and expect abundance—you are just as entitled to it as anyone else and there is plenty to go around.

By repeating positive statements like "I have all the money I need" or "attracting money is easy" over and over again, you'll be imprinting a new message on your subconscious. Take the time to visualise a short film in your mind of how your life would be different if you didn't have to worry over money, and play that film over and over again to yourself. Visualise how you would look if you trusted yourself to provide easily. What would you be doing differently? Would you be more relaxed about the rest of your life? By worrying about just how hard money is to come by or how difficult it is to pay next month's bills, you could be stopping yourself seeing opportunities to earn more or attract money.

My client, Claire, is a self-employed hypnotherapist and a very good one. People come from all over to see her but she told me that, in spite of her success, she is constantly worried about money. When I asked her how much she charged for her sessions, she admitted she was charging less than half her colleagues' rates. When I asked why, the reason was simple—she was scared she'd lose her clientele. I asked Claire to start putting up her prices to new customers. She did and from that moment she attracted a host of new clients. So confident was she after changing her attitude, she is now very happy to turn down those clients that aren't prepared to pay her fees. Claire worked hard to qualify as a hypnotherapist. She spent a lot of money on her training and invested a lot of time in her exams, so she deserves to be recognised both professionally and financially.

Some people I know always keep spare cash in their purse, believing that abundance creates abundance. A friend of mine, Cathy, keeps three one pound coins in a line by her front door. She says it's feng shui for "money in"! Whether you believe or not, maybe it's worth trying?

The truth is that money is not the root of all evil—much good is done with money. Being good and wealthy isn't incompatible. If you honestly believe in your own worth, you will encourage others to believe it too. So do you have a mind to be rich?

Fake it to make it

Are you too shy to make friends? Does the mere thought of public speaking make you feel queasy? This could make all the difference

Do you sometimes wish you were more outgoing? Do you wish you could be the life and soul of the party? Do you cringe with embarrassment at being asked to speak at meetings, give talks or participate in workshops? Well this tip could be exactly what you're looking for.

Ever harboured a secret desire to be an actress? Well, now you can live your dream without the embarrassment of going on stage in front of hundreds. In fact, no one need ever know you're acting.

A client of mine, Adele, works in Customs and Excise and her job is to spot people who may be bringing drugs into the country. When she thinks someone is lying or suspects that their story isn't true, she has to search them. As a female, she is often put in a situation where she has to be confident, strong and persistent, often with men much bigger and stronger than her. Adele has to attend regular self-defence classes to learn how to protect herself properly and do her job safely.

Adele absolutely hates these classes, she cringed and held her head in her hands as she told me that the instructor demonstrates several moves and then, one by one, the students have to perform the moves in front of the rest of the class. This terrifies Adele and she has night-mares about these workshops for weeks before the classes, so I asked her how she would feel if she were auditioning for a film. What if, as part of her audition, she were asked to simulate a struggle and the self-defence move to counteract it. What if it wasn't "her" up there in front of everyone else but her character? What if she was an actress?

She thought for a few minutes, laughed and said that she would probably feel a whole lot better about it. She said that if she was pretending to "act", then it wouldn't really feel so embarrassing.

Adele came back from her workshop absolutely buzzing! Not only had she demonstrated all the moves really well but she hadn't felt anywhere near as nervous as she had done in previous workshops ... so that's the key girls—"act as if".

I have also coached people on how to present themselves at job interviews, on how to meet new friends and overcome shyness, on how to give presentations or appear on TV and how to deal with confrontation more easily. I get brilliant results when I ask people to "act" the part. This tip makes all of these situations much easier to deal with. When you're "acting as if" you can even base your acting skills on a certain actor or character on television. If you're really impressed with the way they handle a certain situation, ask yourself, "What did they do that was so good?" Try to remember how they stood, the phrases they used, their attitude and what they were wearing. This will all help you in your challenge, whatever it is. Whatever you have to do that scares the hell out of you ... pretend you're acting, it really can make all the difference!

Dealing with guilt

Do you end up feeling guilty about everything? Then, this is for you

Suffering from that horrible churning feeling of guilt? The one that, however hard you try, just won't go away? Do you find it difficult to be happy because of something you did or didn't do in your past? This is more common than you think and it could be sorted out faster than you might expect.

Guilt is a horrible feeling. Whether you feel guilty about not attending your best friend's wedding or you still feel guilty about treating someone badly five years ago, the feeling is the same. Women the world over are very good at harbouring guilt regarding just about anything. Because we're so good at it, we really do need to sit ourselves down sometimes and ask ourselves a few questions like "Was it really my fault?" or "Do I really need to feel guilty?" If your

147

stomach turns over at the mere mention of someone's name or a particular incident, then you need to deal with it—now!

Guilt can make you feel very bad and, if allowed to continue, can be the cause of problems both at work and at home. It's time to deal with those guilt pangs and sort them out before they make you ill.

A client of mine, Sally, found herself in a steady, happy relationship but somehow didn't feel as content as she thought she should. When we spoke about it, Sally told me that several years earlier, she had been badly let down by a boyfriend. As a result, she had behaved very badly towards her next partner who had been genuinely kind and caring. He had adored her and treated her like a queen but, for his trouble, she had walked all over his good nature. As a result she felt terribly guilty. I asked her what she needed to do to put things right. She said that she'd need to talk to her ex and apologise for her bad behaviour, so that's exactly what she did. Sally told her new love what she was going to do and, with his blessing, she called her ex-boyfriend. It was a quick phone call but one that cleared the air for both of them. He finally understood some of her actions and she had the chance to apologise. He accepted her apology, that dreadful guilty feeling was lifted and she didn't have to carry it around any more. It was gone for ever and he felt better too.

Is there anyone you need to apologise to? What would it take for you to hold out an olive branch? Has anyone tried to apologise to you and you've not accepted it? Maybe it's time to put the past behind you. Take whatever action you feel is necessary, whether it's a bunch of flowers or writing a well thought out letter. Even if your apology is not accepted, the important thing is that you tried. Don't let guilt bring you down, do what you can and move on.

Lack of time

Are you famous for your "to do" lists? Yearning for a twenty-seven hour day? Read this strategy for coping

Are you always running round like a headless chicken? Does your list of jobs seem never ending? Do you look frazzled and pale at the mere thought of tomorrow and all that it involves? Then breathe deeply and consider this ...

I'd dearly love to know why we can't just invent another few hours in the day. What harm would it really do and whose idea was it to only have twenty-four hours in the first place? The only thing is, though, even if we had twenty- seven hours in a day, I've a sneaking suspicion that we would all still complain about not having enough time. It's a bit like looking into a wardrobe stuffed full of beautiful clothes and screaming, "I've got nothing to wear!"

We've all got someone we could name who runs a household effortlessly, organises really fun things for birthdays, chairs local charity events and works full time; someone who makes us feel totally inadequate. What is it about those people, though, that enables them to do everything so easily and perfectly without ever looking flustered or bleary-eyed through lack of sleep? It's not magic; they haven't got the key to a secret "time bank". They just use their time differently and manage it effectively.

Recently, I asked twenty sixth formers at a local school to add up how much time they thought they spent being unproductive. Being unproductive, I explained, meant watching television rather than getting on with their "to do" list and time spent worrying about how to approach something rather than just getting on with it. Being unproductive meant chatting on the phone for hours to a friend, discussing their life and problems rather than thinking about your own. I've heard some answers before but I really wasn't expecting what they had to say. The worst offender in the group admitted to spending between five and six hours a day being unproductive! Half that time seemed to be spent worrying about the things she had to do and the other half seemed to be spent organising clever little avoidance methods, which she'd got down to a fine art.

Write down how much of your time you spend worrying, avoiding things or watching mind-numbing television just for the sake of it. You might get a shock. The key to being organised, productive and having the time to do everything in a more relaxed manner, is purely to re-arrange the way you spend your time. It is no more complicated than that. Everyone can do it—yes, even you!

Budget your time like you budget your money. Unlike a bank, though, time doesn't have an overdraft—once it's gone, it's gone. Where do you spend your time? How do you spend your time? My client, Becky, has developed a great idea to help save herself time. Before she started her coaching sessions, she would come home from work and put on the television straight away. She'd then kick her shoes off, sit down with a cup of tea and wait for her favourite programme to come on. "Nothing wrong with that," I hear you say? Well, if your favourite programme doesn't come on for another two hours and you're watching things that don't particularly interest you just to pass the time, there could be a problem. That's what Becky realised she was doing—every evening. So she decided to change her habits. She no longer watches television in the week. Becky now records all her favourite programmes throughout the week and sits down on a Sunday to watch the lot. She fast forwards through all the adverts and, if she forgets to set the video, she realises that the programme obviously wasn't very important to her.

Becky goes out more in the evenings and her social life has improved. On the nights she stays in, she listens to music and does all the little jobs around the house that were previously getting out of control. She sews on missing buttons, clears out paperwork—in fact, Becky's evenings have turned into a hive of productivity and she loves it! She told me she thinks she has saved herself over forty hours per week and no longer complains of never having enough time.

My number one tip for those complaining of having too much to do and no time to do it in, is to get themselves an egg timer. This really works: Every second counts and one minute is longer than you think. Here's how to make a huge difference to the state of your home in just thirty minutes. Take your egg timer into a room, set it for five minutes and start tidying up. You'll be amazed at how much you can achieve and how different a room can look and feel in those few minutes. Then, take the egg timer to the next room and do exactly the same. In thirty minutes, you'll have freshened, aired and tidied six rooms!

No one ever said on their death-bed that they wished they'd had time to iron more socks, fold more towels or watch more repeats on television. Go and find that famous "to do" list of yours and halve it! Yep, you did read that right—cross off half those jobs this minute. The chances are you've got far more on there than actually needs to be done. Delegate the jobs that can be done by someone else. Learn to let others help and relinquish some of your control. The world will not stop turning, I promise.

"Yes" v "No"

If you say "yes" to everyone's demands, irrespective of your own plans, saying "no" needn't be as hard as you think—honest!

Do you have problems saying "no"? Are you silently screaming for less demands on your time but taking on more and more regardless? Then it's time to take stock and play a little game.

Women everywhere seem to have problems saying "no". Just two little letters making one small word and we think the world will come to a grinding halt if we utter it. The point is, we know that it won't happen. Our logical brain recognises how crazy this is, nevertheless, whatever the reasoning behind it, we still multi-task. We women have become very adept at juggling a million and one jobs, most of which probably aren't ours, all to avoid those two little letters.

Do *you* find it hard to say "no" to people? Are you someone who finds herself agreeing to all kinds of favours when inside you're thinking, "Just say no!" Well, you're not alone. The problem is when saying "*yes*" has become second nature. If you just can't seem to form the word "*no*" you need to think about this.

From serious issues to minor inconveniences, every time you say "yes" to something, you are actually saying "no" to something else. If you agree to babysit your friends' children, for instance, you could be saying "no" to a night out with friends or a much needed night at home with a glass of wine in front of the television, relaxing in your PJs. Now, if you really want to babysit, hey, go ahead, but if you're dreading the thought, then listen, it is OK to say "no"!

So keen was Sharon to help other people, she nearly put her marriage at risk. I started coaching her when her relationship with her husband had started to deteriorate. He complained that he was spending more and more evenings at home alone with their two-year-old and found it particularly upsetting that their son was in bed by the time she got home. Sharon had a demanding job that took up a lot of her time and energy but, on top of that, she found it incredibly hard to say "no" to people who demanded a share of her time outside work as well. She only realised what she risked losing by saying "yes" to everything when it came to the crunch and she was given an ultimatum.

There are ways of saying "no" though. Most of us are afraid that saying "no" will make us unpopular or look selfish. Then, of course, in comes the usual female guilt about putting yourself first. If you feel under pressure to make a snap decision and feel a definite "yes" coming on, make them wait. Tell them it sounds a great idea and that you'll get back to them. This might sound like a cop out but it will give you chance to work out whether you really do want to do whatever is being asked of you, or not. Work out in your mind exactly what you're missing out on by saying "yes". What are you saying "no" to?

By delaying your response, you will be more prepared to formulate your answer and say "no" with confidence.

Do it now!

Do you constantly put off today what you can do tomorrow? If your "tomorrows" are always a day away, try this tactic

Do you put things off? Things that you really, really don't like doing? Or maybe you put off doing the things that scare you?

This was true of Tamsin. She works for herself so has to make calls to potential clients to generate new business. It became clear during one of our coaching sessions that Tamsin will do absolutely anything rather than make those dreaded phone calls. She felt guilty about not making them and knew that she could get more business if she just plucked up the courage. However, that still wasn't enough of an incentive to make her pick up the phone and start dialling.

Tamsin works from home, so it's really easy to put on the kettle and avoid making her calls. In fact, she was becoming a dab hand at avoiding the issue. She'd put on the washing, hang it out, flick on the news—you get the idea—anything not to pick up the phone. As a result, of course, she had that dreadful nagging feeling in the pit of her stomach every time she thought about her list of calls. When we spoke about what it was that stopped her calling people her answer was: fear of rejection. What if they didn't remember her? What if they didn't want to use her work? How embarrassing would that be? It was only when we talked about it that she realised the embarrassment (if indeed there was anything to be embarrassed about) would last only as long as the call. The calls were to people that she either didn't know very well or didn't know at all, so what was there to be embarrassed about? Tamsin told me that when she does pluck up the courage to call people, they are generally very nice to her and, as a result, subsequent phone calls aren't difficult at all—it's the first call that's the hardest one.

After talking about it, Tamsin did say that she felt much better about making that initial call but I wasn't convinced that she felt confident enough to make them when she had no one there to chivvy her along. I asked her what she would need to do to make herself pick up the phone when she was feeling least like it. She said that she would just have to make herself do it—perhaps say to herself, "Do it now!" In reality, though, that's hard to remember, so Tamsin agreed to type a big sign saying "DO IT NOW!" and stick it above her desk. Guess what … it worked.

Tamsin made the phone calls she had been dreading and of course they were nowhere near as difficult as she thought they might be. So, take a leaf out of Tamsin's book and work out exactly what would make you do the things that you most dread doing. Do you need a sign of your own? What would it say and where would you put it? Sometimes, we are the only ones that can give ourselves the encouragement we need, so whatever it is, do it now— your way.

Do you believe in fairies?

Always left with the chores and getting fed up? Stop moaning and start believing in this fairytale

Are you ever accused of nagging? Are you fed up with the sound of your own voice moaning that you seem to be the only one who knows where the washing machine is and how it works? Getting frustrated that the mere mention of the washing-up puts the rest of your family into some kind of panic? Then you obviously don't have fairies at home ... read on, because this tip works a treat.

When I ask my clients to start believing in fairies, they think I'm losing the plot!

The inspiration for this tip came from my parents. As children, my brother Craig and I lived with fairies. There was the Lynette fairy who was responsible for all the naughty things that Lynette did and didn't own up to and then there was the Craig fairy who, if my memory serves me right, was *always* in trouble (sorry bro!). Now I have my own house, Nick and I have fairies too, lots of them! We have the washing-up fairy, the laundry fairy, the bathroom fairy, the tidying-up fairy, we even have the dog-walking fairy and they work like this. On my way out of the door, if the washing-up has been staring me in the face for a while, I'll ask Nick to give the washing-up fairy a quick call and see if she's coming into work today. In short that really means, "Darling, make sure that washing-up is done by the time I get home or there'll be trouble," or it might mean, "You've not cleared up the kitchen once this week and you're really starting to get on my nerves". Getting the picture? You see, fairies take the anger out of a situation. They take the blame directly off the other person and put it on to a third party, albeit a third party that doesn't really exist. (Actually, some of my clients do start to believe in fairies, but that's a different story!)

If either one of us feels they are doing more than their fair share of the housework, we have been known to get a bit sarcastic about the fairies. We'll comment on how they call in sick for instance or even forget to come to work at all and, if either one of us breaks something then, you guessed it, it was probably the fairies!

Instead of a household chore causing an argument, the fairies just make us laugh, the person in the wrong gets the point and guess what … the fairies arrive for work. So if your family is starting to treat you like their number one slave and you're getting fed up, introduce them to the fairies. Start believing … and you never know what might happen.

Feeling blurry?

Lacking energy and enthusiasm? Kick start your body—this tip couldn't be simpler

Do you wake up most days feeling as if you're not quite with it? Do you get the sense that, any time now, you could develop a major headache? Not quite feeling one hundred per cent? This tip is something everyone should know about. Tell your friends, too.

There is a condition that nearly everyone suffers from at some point during the day and it can make you feel lousy. You can lose your concentration and forget things, it can induce headaches, make you feel irritated and tired and you can even lose your libido. The problem is dehydration and the cure is simple. It's water.

Before I can help my clients tackle their problems or achieve their goals, they need to be in a receptive state of mind, and part of that means making sure they are hydrated and know the symptoms of dehydration. In my opinion, if my clients are constantly dehydrated, they are starting off with one huge disadvantage. The body can get dehydrated very quickly, depending on what you're doing, but one thing you should know is that thirst is a poor indicator of a state of dehydration. By the time your body tells you that you're thirsty, you are already dehydrated and you may well be suffering some of the above symptoms.

The best way to make sure that your body keeps hydrated is to drink small glasses of water very regularly. Keep a bottle with you and fill it up throughout the day. If you find it difficult to remember to drink water, then link it with something else you do regularly.

Dawn came to see me when she wanted to make changes in her life but didn't seem able to get any of them off the ground. She felt tired all the time, had no energy to fulfil her plans and her enthusiasm and confidence were disappearing fast. I asked her about her life and her future plans, but I also asked how much water she drank each day. "None" was the answer. Dawn said she never even thought of drinking plain water and tended to stick to coffee or tea. I explained that her tiredness could be due to the fact that she was dehydrated and that if she was going to start making changes in her life, she would need to start taking better care of her body. Dawn agreed to drink eight tumblers of water each day. A tumbler is roughly half a pint of water, so Dawn was committing herself to drinking at least four pints a day. That sounds a lot but if you link it to something you do regularly, then it really isn't that much. For instance, if you drink your first glass after brushing your teeth, have a glass with your lunch, a glass with your dinner and a glass before you go to bed, that's four glasses already. Dawn was quite sure she couldn't give up her tea and coffee, so she agreed to drink a glass of water either before or after each cup of tea and coffee.

I saw Dawn a month later and she felt a lot better. She had kept her promise to drink her eight tumblers of water and had even started to notice when her body was dehydrating. One of the biggest changes I noticed was that her eyes were blue. I hadn't noticed the first time we met, but this time, they really stood out. They were clear, shiny and very, very blue. Dawn told me that she felt much more positive and energised about starting her life coaching and felt ready to redirect her future.

If you're suffering from any of the symptoms described in this tip, do make sure you get them checked out by your doctor or an alternative practitioner but, do not underestimate how important drinking water is to the smooth running of our bodies. Drinking water is a habit that you need to adopt. Don't wait until your body is crying out. Keep it topped up and you'll be less stressed, more in control and far more productive—you could also be a nicer person to be around.

Winter blues

Perk up those down days with a little imagination

Do you find you get easily depressed in winter? Do you find yourself hibernating and feeling dreadful when it's cold, wet and windy outside? Well, put an end to the winter blues and follow this tip.

Good old winter: some days are gloriously sunny, chilly and crisp—they can be absolutely beautiful. Those are the days that fill you with inspiration and joy, but most of our winter days really do seem very, very dreary. From early morning it's grey, the lights are on by mid-afternoon and the day hardly seems to get going before it's pitch-black again and you're struggling home through windy, wet streets. Winter starts so early and seems to go on for an eternity. It's an absolute nightmare if you're the type of person whose mood seems to be dictated by the weather.

If that's you, then it's time to listen to your body and pander to its needs.

I apologise if you're reading this and it's twenty-eight degrees in the shade but read on anyway, this could still affect you and the summer is a great time to take action.

You know when, in the depths of winter, sometimes you wake up and just want to disappear under the covers again? Traditionally, it's known as the winter blues. You're feeling awful and crying at the drop of a hat. It's raining and windy outside and you're bored stiff but feeling worse for staying indoors. You turn on the television and there's nothing remotely interesting to watch. Probably the whole house could be cleaned and tidied. The cupboards should be cleared out and reorganised and then there's the washing. These days though are strictly for self-indulgence. Use this tip to spoil yourself and turn a potentially disastrous day into the best day you've had this year.

Without sounding like a children's television programme, all you need is an empty box and some imagination. You're going to put together a *winter box*. You'll open this box when those winter blues kick in. This is the box that you'll love and be thankful for when life seems like an uphill struggle, it's your winter blues box and the idea came from Victoria.

Victoria came to see me in winter. She told me that she always felt so awful at this time of year. On the days she absolutely had to go to work, she dragged herself in with no make-up, looking a mess. On her days off, if the blues struck, she knew it was going to be a boring, upsetting and unproductive time. She explained that, by the time she gets to the end of a day like this, she starts to feel a bit better and comes up with 101 things she could have done to cheer herself up, but of course, by then, it's too late. The day has been a disaster.

I asked her what she could do to turn those awful days into wonderful moments of sheer pleasure. I love the answer she gave and I've used it with lots of clients since. Victoria said that she would put together a winter blues box. On a day when she was feeling energetic and positive, Victoria would go shopping for things to fill her box with, things that made her feel special. On her list would be: scented candles, expensive bubble bath, a face pack, a good book, her favourite PJs, a feel-good video, some handmade chocolates and a note to herself reminding her that this feeling wouldn't last for ever. From that moment on, she made a promise to us both that she would use these days to take time to look after herself properly.

This really works. Victoria put her box together with winter in mind, but you can use this tip at any time of year. We all get down days where we can't be bothered to do anything, but instead of feeling sorry for yourself, make up a little box of treasures and treat yourself. What would you have in yours?

Single again and scared stiff!

Divorced? Separated? Single? A woman's guide to feeling whole again

Is fear of being single keeping you in a bad relationship? Are you finding it hard to face life on your own? Then take strength from this.

Being single after years of being part of a couple is often a frightening prospect. Whether it's your decision to break up or not, it changes everything about who you are and who you thought you were. Friends suddenly disappear, people look at you in a different light and you need to rely on your inner reserve of energy and determination to get you through.

If you've suddenly been dumped, you'll have had a picture in your mind of how your life was going to be and, when it all comes crashing down, you either sink or swim.

Be determined to swim and you could discover a whole new you.

Isobel came to see me after having been through a break up with her partner. The split had been her decision and she knew that being on her own was the healthier option, but it meant she was entering a completely new world. Isobel had never really been single, she'd always had someone to go places with and felt very odd about suddenly having to do everything on her own.

Determined to structure a new life for herself, she started with her biggest fear, walking into a bar on her own. We talked about the best way to conquer her fear and she decided to tackle it head on. There was a brand new wine bar that had opened not far from her house and she said she'd love to go there, so she did, on her own. Armed with a glossy magazine for security, Isobel got dressed up, walked into the wine bar and sat and ate a bowl of strawberries with a glass of champagne—now that's what I call overcoming a fear with style! Well, it worked. No one really took much notice of her and she certainly didn't feel as if she was being stared at. She didn't feel like she hadn't got any friends and she didn't feel as though she'd been stood up. That day made a massive difference to Isobel's confidence because she realised that she was perfectly capable of building herself a new life alone.

One of my other clients, Cara, spoke to me a few months ago. After being in a marriage for over ten years, she found herself on her own having to bring up three children. She told me that there was always so much noise in the house that she would have to shout to be heard above the children to try to get them to calm down and be nice to each other. Minutes later, the house would be in uproar again until she couldn't take any more and ended up in tears. Of course, every time Cara cried, the children felt awful and a dreadful sense of sadness filled the house, leaving her feeling like a bad mother who had no control over her kids. With no one at home to back her up, we needed to get Cara to regroup her family and feel in control again. We spoke about two ways of achieving her objective.

The first was to come up with a pre-agreed physical signal for Cara's children to react to when they got too noisy and started fighting. Instead of standing at their bedroom door and shouting over their noise, Cara agreed to stand there and just raise her arm. This would be the children's new sign that they were going too far and that they needed to calm down. She decided to use it as a warning before she got to the stage of shouting or crying and agreed to sit down and talk this through with them.

The second way of regrouping the family was for Cara to come up with a set of family values with her children. You've already read about how your personal values can help you focus on your direction. Well, by asking the children to come up with their own set of values to live by they were, in effect, creating for themselves a set of rules to follow. Most families have values, but they don't necessarily spell them out. Cara agreed to sit down with her children and come up with the values that meant a lot to them. When they had their top three, Cara would get the children to create a poster to put up in the kitchen where everyone could see them.

When the children were rude to each other and started to get out of control, instead of telling them off, Cara agreed to ask them if they were respecting their family values. She felt that her children were old enough to start respecting other people's values and was very eager to teach her children this new exercise.

Finding yourself with the sole responsibility of children and bills is frightening. It's about becoming independent, not relying on others for lifts, money or favours. It's about standing on your own two feet and trusting that you'll make it. Cara needed to redefine not only who she was as a woman but who and what her family stood for.

Like Cara, after years spent being part of a couple, Isobel had to recreate her own identity. She changed the way she dressed, she redecorated her house in the colours she loved, she changed the locks on the front door and she always made her own way to places so she could leave when she wanted. Isobel started to feel in control of her new life, as did Cara.

Even something as small as changing the message on the answer phone is a very positive start. Big lessons are learnt when two becomes one: the pain fades, a new life emerges and the very best revenge is success, so have a little faith in yourself, you'll be just fine.

When I feel stressed I ...

Do you really know how stress affects you? How would you love your family and friends to treat you when you feel stressed? Maybe it's time to spell it out

How does stress affect you? Do you get headaches? Maybe you cry or get angry? Recognise when your body tells you to de-stress and you'll be the one in control.

Stress is a much overused word in my view and it seems that everyone is concerned about being stressed. However, stress isn't necessarily a bad thing. A degree of pressure in our lives is actually very normal and vital to the smooth running of our bodies. Stress can be very powerful, though, and so needs to be respected and managed effectively. It is only when stress is not handled correctly and sensibly that it can become detrimental to your health and wellbeing.

Physiologically, stress is a primitive response in everybody. When we perceive a situation as potentially threatening, our adrenal glands spring into action and adrenalin, our fight/flight hormone, is produced to help us cope with this threat.

Ideally, when we've coped with a stressful event, it would be brilliant if we could ensure the next few days were calm so we could let our bodies get back into balance and feel relaxed again. Of course, life doesn't always let us do that. When we are under long-term stress and feel unable to relax at all, our bodies and emotions can start to feel the strain. Different people feel different symptoms of stress and any of these could be a first sign—feeling snappy and irritable, getting small inconsequential things out of all proportion, getting more headaches than usual, feeling sick, losing your appetite or constantly comfort eating. Which one rings a bell with you? It is really important to know when your body is under stress so you can try to build in some relaxation time. If you know that your shoulders and neck muscles tense up with stress, don't just work through it, do something about it.

Figure out what your stress warning signs are and tell the people around you. Don't just carry on, expecting your body and mind to live up to supernatural standards. Listen to the signs and take them as a signal to slow down.

When you get stressed, what would be the best way for your friends and family to treat you? What is the best thing for you to do with yourself when it all gets a bit much? Sue, a client of mine, knows that, after a stressful day at work, she really needs to be alone for a while to unwind. Her family understand that she's not upset with them and she's not avoiding them, they just know to leave her be until she's had a shower, taken off her make-up and is feeling fresher again. After that, Sue wants to know all about their day, what they've been up to and, finally, she can start to think about what to cook for dinner.

What is it that you need to do to de-stress? Explain to your family how you want them to treat you. Do you want to be left alone? Do you want a hug and some attention? Having an action plan in place will mean that you are better equipped to cope and you'll feel much calmer, much sooner. So do yourself a favour and finish off these sentences:

When I feel stressed I …
From now on, when I feel stressed I will …
My friends/family can help me by …

Make those you live and work with aware of how you'd like to be treated when you're feeling fragile. Tell them that, even though you're snapping at them, they probably haven't done anything wrong. Explain what's going on when you're stressed and your world will become a much better place!

My letter to you ...

Lights, camera, action!

I've loved putting this book together. I've thought long and hard about its content and the people whose stories I have shared with you. If, by reading it, I have inspired you to change the way you do something, alter the way you think about yourself or dare to believe that there is more inside you than you previously thought, then I've done the very best I can for you.

You've read the tips, you've learnt a bit about how the subconscious mind works, you've looked at the ideas on intuition and learned how you can rely on it to direct your life, so use all this information wisely. Don't just put this book down and forget what you've read, use your intuition more, make a friend of your subconscious and make sure that every part of your life is just as you would love it to be.

If, as a result of reading *Behind with the Laundry and Living off Chocolate*, you've put any of these strategies into action in order to change something in your life to make it more fulfilling, more exciting or more stress-free, then you need to be congratulated! You can read a thousand books and talk to a million people but unless you are prepared to change the way you do things, you won't benefit from any of them. This stuff is truly valuable. Make it your own, alter it to fit into your schedule and put your own personal twist on it. Use these ideas and let my clients' stories inspire you.

The accounts in this book are real. The women you have read about have been strong enough not only to visualise what they want, but they have also been determined enough to put their trust in themselves. Because of that, they feel more enriched, more satisfied, more in control and less guilty! Every woman deserves to be loved, to feel loved and to feel special. Every woman deserves the right to be true to herself and to fulfil her passions as an individual. Real women have the strength to know when to walk away, when to stay and fight, when it's worth it and when it's not. Trust your decisions and trust that whatever happens, you'll be OK.

We have the gift of communication, the ability to reach more people every day than we realise. Think about what you say to yourself and those around you. Think about who influences you, who you influence, who you teach and what you are teaching because, in every single behaviour pattern you use, someone else learns through you. People admire you, so go ahead and enjoy being admired. Living a fulfilling life is precious and the mind and body you inhabit are under your control.

Take action today, any kind of action, stand up for yourself, be the woman you want to be. You know and understand the strength of being a woman and having it all. It's already yours.

Lynette x

To contact me for more information or to comment on any of the tips in this book, visit *www.lynetteallen.co.uk*

Behind with the Laundry and Living off Chocolate
Life changing strategies for busy women

Tracklist for accompanying CD

1. How well do you take care of yourself? **06:11**
2. "I am calm" **01:08**
3. Say what you mean **02:49**
4. Buying time for busy women **01:47**
5. Watch out—subconscious at work **05:54**
6. Eliminate problems! **03:28**
7. Ask the question **01:25**
8. Go on, flex those muscles! **04:27**
9. Set boundaries and find your parallel universe! **05:12**
10. Directionally challenged? **02:31**
11. The High/Low game **02:20**
12. When I feel stressed I … **03:39**